Predicting External Imbalances for the United States and Japan

WILLIAM R. CLINE

Predicting External Imbalances for the United States and Japan

Institute for International Economics
Washington, DC
September 1995

William R. Cline, *Senior Fellow,* was formerly a Senior Fellow at the Brookings Institution (1973–81); Deputy Director for Development and Trade Research in Brazil (1971–73); Ford Foundation Visiting Professor in Brazil (1970–71) and Assistant Professor at Princeton University (1967–70). His numerous books include *International Debt Reexamined* (1995), *The Economics of Global Warming* (1992), *The Future of World Trade in Textiles and Apparel* (revised edition 1990), *United States External Adjustment and the World Economy* (1989), *International Debt: Systemic Risk and Policy Response* (1984), *Trade Policy in the 1980s* (1984), *World Inflation and the Developing Countries* (1981), and *Trade Negotiations in the Tokyo Round* (1978).

INSTITUTE FOR INTERNATIONAL ECONOMICS
11 Dupont Circle, NW
Washington, DC 20036-1207
(202) 328-9000 FAX: (202) 328-0900

C. Fred Bergsten, *Director*
Christine F. Lowry, *Director of Publications*

Typesetting by Automated Graphic Systems
Printing by Automated Graphic Systems

Printed in the United States of America
97 96 95 5 4 3 2 1

Library of Congress Cataloging-in-Publication Data

Cline, William R.
Predicting external imbalances for the United States and Japan / William R. Cline.
p. cm. — (Policy analyses in international economics ; 41) Includes bibliographical references.
1. Balance of trade—United States.
2. United States—Commercial policy.
3. Japan—Commerce—United States.
4. United States—Commerce—Japan.
I. Title. II. Series.
HF3031.C55 1995 95-33350
382′.17′ 0973—dc20 CIP

ISBN 0-88132-220-2

Marketed and Distributed outside the USA and Canada by Longman Group UK Limited, London

ents

Preface vii

Acknowledgments xi

1 Introduction 1

2 A Reduced Form Model of the Current Account 7
Specifying the Trade Equations 7
Data Base 16
Trade Ratio Estimation Results 21
Factor Services and Transfers 26
Current Account Model and Backcasts 31

3 Current Account Forecasts 39
Has the Dollar Collapsed? 39
Qualitative Outlook 41
Forecast Assumptions 42
The Mexico Factor 43
A Consensus Model 44
EAG Model 46
Projections 46
Impact Parameters 49

4 Conclusion 59
Implications of the Analysis 59
Overview 73

Appendix 75
Technical Note 1: Supply and Demand in the Trade Equations 75
Technical Note 2: Pass-through Estimates 76

References 79

Figures
1 United States: trade ratio and real exchange rate, 1980–94 3
2 Japan: trade ratio and real exchange rate, 1980–94 4
3 United States real effective exchange rates: developed versus less developed countries, 1976–second quarter 1995 17
4 Japanese real effective exchange rate, 1978–first quarter 1995 18
5 United States: RFM backcasts of trade ratios for trade with developed countries 25
6 United States: RFM backcasts of trade ratios for trade with developing countries 26
7 Japan: RFM backcasts of trade ratios 26
8 United States: exports of goods and nonfactor services to developed and developing countries, quarterly, 1978–94 27
9 Japan: exports of goods and nonfactor services, 1980–94 28
10 United States and Japan: factor services income and payments, 1980–93 30
11 United States and Japan: net factor services, 1980–94 30
12 United States: net transfers, 1980–94 31
13 United States: actual and predicted current account, 1983–94 37
14 Japan: actual and predicted current account, 1983–94 37
15 United States: RFM consensus model backcast of trade ratio 46
16 United States: bilateral trade balances, 1980–94 65
17 Fiscal adjustment, expectations, and the exchange rate 67
18 Fiscal and current account deficits 68

Tables
1 Regression results 22
2 Linear time trend equations 29
3 United States: actual and predicted current account, 1980–94 33
4 Japan: actual and predicted current account, 1980–94 35
5 Alternative current account projections, 1994–97 47
6 Impact parameters: RFM, CNS, and EAG models 52

Preface

The Institute has devoted considerable attention to analyzing the causes of changes in national trade balances and current account positions, the impact of changes in exchange rates on these variables, and thus the appropriateness of particular currency levels. Our recent studies on these topics include Paul Krugman's *Has the Adjustment Process Worked?* (October 1991), my own *International Adjustment and Financing: The Lessons of 1985–1991* (January 1992), John Williamson's *Estimating Equilibrium Exchange Rates* (September 1994) and William Cline's *United States External Adjustment and the World Economy* (May 1989).

The Institute has also paid particular attention to the evolution of these issues in the two largest economies in the world: the United States and Japan. In addition to the studies cited above, Stephen Marris addressed the American situation in *Deficits and the Dollar: The World Economy at Risk* (2d ed., November 1987), and I did so in *America in the World Economy* (March 1988). Bela Balassa and Marcus Noland analyzed *Japan in the World Economy* (1988), and Noland and I looked at the interrelationships between the two countries in *Reconcilable Differences? United States-Japan Economic Conflict* (June 1993).

This new study by William Cline takes a fresh look at the American and Japanese imbalances, their likely future course in light of recent changes in exchange rates and in their domestic economies, and the implications thereof for both. To do so, he has developed a new and deliberately simple model, which—while also being compared against more elaborate earlier models, including his own—can be deployed rapidly and easily to update the findings included here. Because of the potential utility of the model itself, as well as its simplicity, we include more of the statistical methodology in this release than is usual for Institute publications. The reader who is not interested in the analytical details can skip chapter 2 and proceed directly to Dr. Cline's findings in chapter 3 and conclusions in chapter 4.

The Institute for International Economics is a private nonprofit institution for the study and discussion of international economic policy. Its purpose is to analyze important issues in that area and to develop and communicate practical new approaches for dealing with them. The Institute is completely nonpartisan.

The Institute is funded largely by philanthropic foundations. Major institutional grants are now being received from the German Marshall Fund of the United States, which created the Institute with a generous commitment of funds in 1981, and from the Ford Foundation, the William M. Keck, Jr. Foundation, the Korea Foundation, the Andrew Mellon Foundation, the C. V. Starr Foundation, and the United States–Japan Foundation. A number of other foundations and private corporations also contribute to the highly diversified financial resources of the Institute. About 12 percent of the Institute's resources in our latest fiscal year were provided by contributors outside the United States, including about 5 percent from Japan.

The Board of Directors bears overall responsibility for the Institute and gives general guidance and approval to its research program—including identification of topics that are likely to become important to international economic policymakers over the medium run (generally, one to three years), and which thus should be addressed by the Institute. The Director, working closely with the staff and outside Advisory Committee, is responsible for the development of particular projects and makes the final decision to publish an individual study.

The Institute hopes that its studies and other activities will contribute to building a stronger foundation for international economic policy around the world. We invite readers of these publications to let us know how they think we can best accomplish this objective.

C. Fred Bergsten
Director
August 1995

INSTITUTE FOR INTERNATIONAL ECONOMICS
11 Dupont Circle, NW, Washington, DC 20036-1207
(202) 328-9000 Fax: (202) 328-0900

Acknowledgments

I am grateful to C. Fred Bergsten, Jaime Marquez, Jeffrey Frankel, Morris Goldstein, Edward M. Graham, Peter Hooper, Marcus Noland, J. David Richardson, Edwin C. Truman, and John Williamson for helpful comments, and exonerate them from responsibility for my views and for any remainng errors. My thanks also go to Albert Y. Kim for research assistance and to Kerry Lecky for typing.

1

Introduction

In the mid-1980s, the United States ran huge trade and current account deficits while Germany and Japan incurred huge surpluses. The US current account deficit reached $164 billion in 1987, or 3.6 percent of GDP, and the surpluses of Germany and Japan reached the range of 4 percent of GDP. Overvaluation of the dollar through early 1985 was the driving force of the US imbalance, and the dollar's subsequent decline—aided importantly by the Plaza Agreement of September 1985—was the most important element in reducing the US deficit (although US recession in the early 1990s was, unfortunately, another factor).

The US current account deficit fell to a low of $7 billion in 1991 (when it probably would have been about $50 billion—or slightly less than 1 percent of GDP—in the absence of special payments received for US efforts in the Gulf War). Since then the large deficits have reemerged. In 1994 alone the deficit rose from $104 billion to $156 billion. The widening of the deficit was associated with a period of renewed tension in US trade relations with Japan, where the current account surplus was similarly headed back toward a relatively large $130 billion after having fallen as low as $36 billion in 1990.

Then in early 1995, there was a sharp decline of the dollar against the yen especially but also against the deutsche mark. The overall result was that after having been quiescent for nearly a decade, the problem of external imbalances and corresponding currency turmoil seemed to be back near the top of the policy agenda.

The reappearance of serious external imbalances for the United States and Japan heightened the importance of timely and reliable forecasts of the external accounts. In particular, by early 1995 it was of great policy importance to know whether the dollar had fallen too far, as averred in April by the Group of Seven finance ministers and the IMF's managing director at the Interim Committee meetings and again in June at the G-7 Summit in Halifax, Canada. Correspondingly, it was important to know whether there was a large adjustment in the US current account deficit in the pipeline as a result of the seemingly large fall in the dollar. Ironically, by the time this study went to press in mid-August 1995, there had been a major rally in the dollar against the yen and deutsche mark, raising the issue of whether the medium-term current account outlook for the United States was one of wider rather than narrowing imbalances.

This study emerged as an effort to answer these questions. The author's earlier multicountry model (Cline 1989) provided one basis for doing so. However, it seemed appropriate to develop a parallel, streamlined model that could provide an additional basis for forecasting, to serve both as an independent check on the multicountry model and as a vehicle for obtaining early answers pending full reestimation and updating of that model. At the same time, it seemed useful to add to the existing stable of models a new entry that could be supple and simple, yet accurate.

Forecasting models of the external current account typically involve numerous equations and intensive data requirements. Thus, the principal model used by the US Federal Reserve to project the US current account (Helkie and Hooper 1988) employs over 400 equations. For its part, the External Adjustment with Growth (EAG) model developed in Cline (1989) applies trade equations for the world divided into 17 major countries and regions. In principle, such models require detailed information often available only with substantial lags, so in practice forecasts often must make do with approximations. Estimation of structural parameters is an extensive undertaking, so there is a tendency to apply ad hoc adjustment factors as the model becomes dated rather than to update parameter estimates comprehensively.[1]

This study seeks to exploit a vivid empirical relationship between trade performance and the real exchange rate to obtain a simple forecasting model that is at once accurate in backcasting (i.e., replicating past current account developments) and lenient in data requirements. The empirical relationship is that the ratio of the value of imports to the value of exports, appropriately defined to remove nongermane factors (mainly oil price shocks), responds strongly to the real exchange rate after a time lag, usually about two years. Cline (1991b, 19) showed this close relationship for the United States during 1980–90; and Cline (1993, 6–7; 1994, 89–90) showed a similar relationship for Japan at both the aggregate level and for bilateral trade with the United States.

---

1. Cline (1991a) discusses rebasing the EAG model through the use of bilateral trade scalars increasing or shrinking model estimates to conform with the most recent observations.

Figure 1 United States: trade ratio and real exchange rate, 1980–94

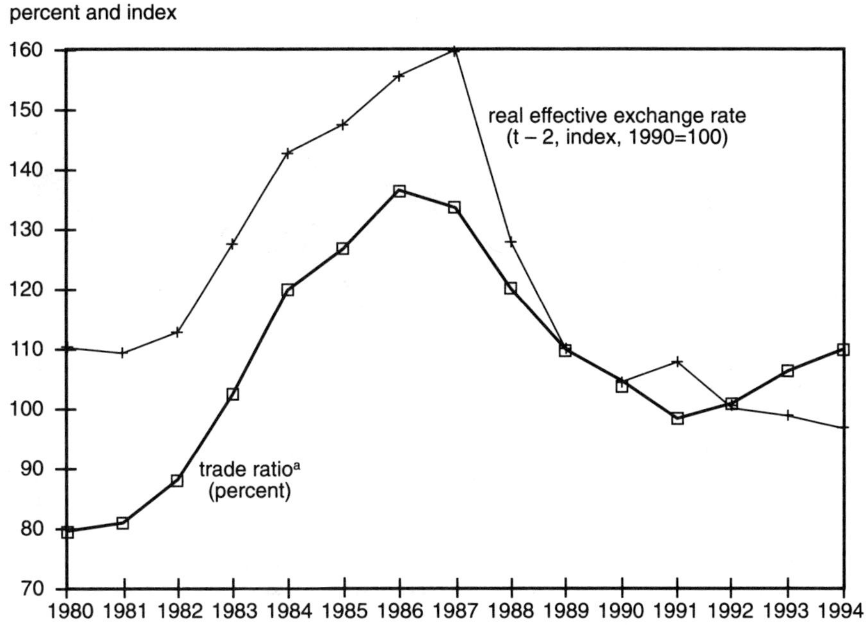

a. Nonoil imports of goods and nonfactor services over exports of goods and nonfactor services.

Figures 1 and 2 show that this strong empirical relationship holds for total trade of both the United States and Japan, for the full period 1980–94. In these presentations, the numerator of the trade ratio is the value of nonoil imports of goods and nonfactor services. The denominator is the value of exports of goods and nonfactor services. The real exchange rate variable is plotted for the observation two years earlier, the idea being that the lags for recognition, ordering, and delivering cumulate to a period centered at two years. The real exchange rate series used here is the International Monetary Fund's real effective exchange rate (REER) and reflects real appreciation when the index is higher.[2] The two curves (trade ratio and real exchange rate) adhere closely for both countries, supporting the idea that the real exchange rate signal has an important impact on subsequent trade performance.

The model developed here first estimates equations relating the trade ratios shown in figures 1 and 2 to the real exchange rates shown in the figures as well as to activity variables and nominal exchange rates (which are relevant to the "pass-through" of exchange rate changes as discussed

2. This series, reported on each country page of *International Financial Statistics,* is calculated deflating by unit-value labor costs in manufacturing across 21 industrial nations.

Figure 2 Japan: trade ratio and real exchange rate, 1980–94

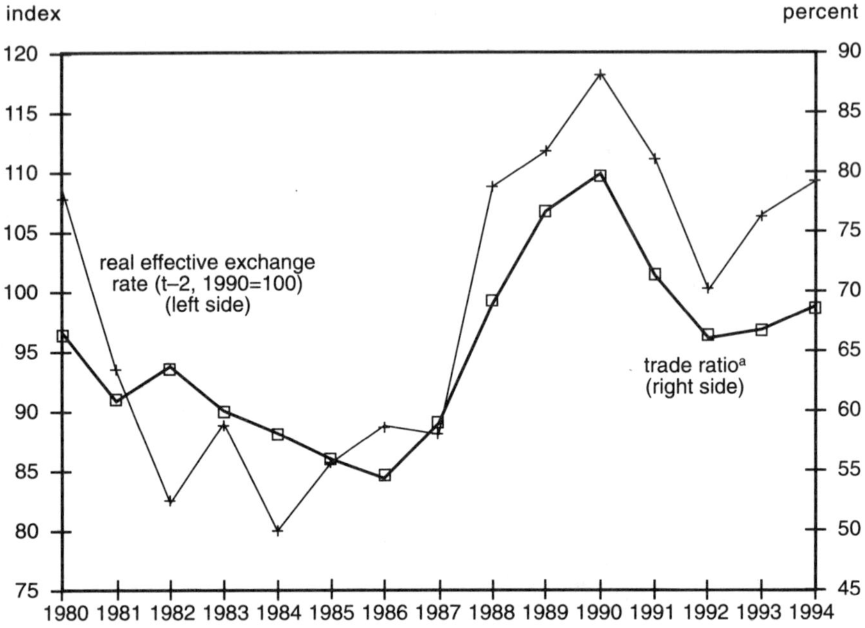

a. Nonoil imports of goods and nonfactor services over exports of goods and nonfactor services.

below). For the United States, the model is specified separately for trade with industrial countries and developing countries, using a different real exchange rate series for the latter group. The trade ratio equations then provide the centerpiece of a simple current account forecasting model that relies on linear time trends for the other elements of the current account. Because the value magnitudes for trade in goods and services are much larger than the magnitudes for other elements of the accounts (factor services balances, transfers), the swings in the differences between the import and export estimates should provide the bulk of the information about the swings in the current account balance. As a result, conducting behavioral equation estimates only for the trade ratio and relying on trends for the other elements should provide a good approximation of the overall account.

There are, of course, both disadvantages and advantages of constructing a simple, streamlined model of the type proposed here. The opposite extreme may be found in large, macroeconomic, general equilibrium models (such as those used for policy regime simulations in Bryant, Hooper, and Mann 1993). Such models can trace the influences from, and feedbacks to, underlying macroeconomic variables such as interest rates, inflation, and growth in examining external accounts. In contrast, even the large "partial equilibrium" models (such as Helkie and Hooper 1988) take the key macroeconomic variables as given and calculate the resulting paths that may be expected for external accounts. Interestingly, official entities charged with forecasting often seem to rely more on the "workhorse" partial equilibrium models than on the more sophisticated general equilibrium models for predicting trends in external balances.[3]

In the choice between partial equilibrium and general equilibrium, transparency and even accuracy of backcasts can favor the former—as models for predicting results from proximate causes—even if intellectual satisfaction and the ability to trace outcomes back to ultimate causes might favor the latter. In the choice between large and small models, nuance and completeness will tend to favor the former, but transparency, ease of data preparation, and timeliness of results can favor the latter.

The Reduced Form Model (RFM) developed in this study is squarely in the category of the small, partial equilibrium model. As such, it may be of particular relevance to private-sector forecasters and to policymakers with frontline responsibilities, as opposed to those in environments that allow for more leisurely paced but more comprehensive analyses.

Chapter 2 of this study derives the equations used to obtain statistical estimates of trade behavior in the model, discusses the data employed, reviews the resulting parameter estimates, and adds the time trends for nontrade components of the current account. Chapter 3 shows the performance of the model in explaining the current account over the past dozen years, develops the forecasts of this study, and calibrates the impact of alternative exchange rate and economic growth assumptions on the current account estimates. Chapter 4 sets forth the major findings of the study.

---

3. Thus, in the International Monetary Fund the individual current account forecasts for major countries reported in the *World Economic Outlook* tend to be from the relevant regional or country desks, using partial equilibrium models and judgmental adjustments. The IMF's general equilibrium macroeconomic model, MULTIMOD (Masson, Symansky, and Meredith 1990), tends instead to be reserved for conducting counterfactual simulations against these baselines.

2

A Reduced Form Model of the Current Account

Specifying the Trade Equations

To determine the proper specification of estimating equations designed to capture the empirical relationships in figures 1 and 2, it is necessary first to consider the underlying behavior of imports and exports. The standard form of a trade equation relates the trade *volume* to the real exchange rate, with some lag structure, and to an activity variable, usually in the current period. The real exchange rate represents the price of domestic supply relative to foreign supply and equals the domestic price times the nominal exchange rate, divided by the foreign price (in foreign currency). Thus, for a given period *t*:

$$R^* = \frac{P_d}{P_f} R \qquad (1)$$

In equation 1, if one is considering US imports from Germany (for example), imports will be more attractive when the domestic price (P_d) is high, the number of deutsche marks per dollar, or R, is high, and the German deutsche mark price (P_f) is low. That is, all three influences make the real exchange rate R^* high.

At the same time, exporters in each country may only "pass through" part of the exchange rate change to their export price. In the appreciating country, the exporter may cut profit margins to remain competitive. In the depreciating country, the exporter may take advantage of the depreciation to raise prices and profit margins, partially offsetting the depreciation. Then the traded-goods prices do not strictly accompany the price in the domestic market, so it is necessary to consider not only the domestic prices and the nominal exchange rate, but also the degree of pass-through in obtaining the price relevant for trade. The trade prices are then:

$$P_x = P_d R^{\epsilon} \tag{2}$$

$$P_m = P_f R^{\rho} \tag{3}$$

In equation 2, the export price equals the domestic price multiplied by a function of the nominal exchange rate. The exponent on the exchange rate, ϵ, tells the extent to which exporters change prices to partially offset the direct effect of the exchange rate change. For example, if exporters reduce prices by one-tenth of the exchange rate appreciation, then $\epsilon = -0.1$. If pass-through is complete, there is no offsetting response to the exchange rate movement, $\epsilon = 0$, and the final term in equation 2 becomes unity so that export price simply equals domestic price.

Similarly, in equation 3, import price (P_m) depends on the foreign price (P_f) in the foreign currency and on the exchange rate of foreign currency per unit of domestic currency (R). If there is complete pass-through, this relationship is a simple currency translation: $P_m = P_f/R$, and the coefficient ρ is simply -1. However, when foreign exporters react to a depreciation of the dollar (for example) by reducing their prices and creating a wedge between their home-market prices (P_f) and their export prices (P_m from the US standpoint), the coefficient ρ will be smaller (in absolute value) than unity. For example, if a 10 percent depreciation of the dollar induces foreign exporters to cut their home-currency prices in the US market by 2 percent, the US import price will rise by only 8 percent, and the import price pass-through coefficient ρ will be only -0.8.[1]

Trade is also influenced by activity levels, so that the basic trade equation relates the volume of trade to the lagged real trade price and the level of real GDP at home (for import demand) or abroad (for export demand). Designating the lag structure for prices by the subscript L, we then have the two central equations for the volume of exports and imports.

$$X^q = \alpha \left[\frac{P_x R}{P_f} \right]_L^{\beta} Y_f^{\gamma} \tag{4}$$

$$M^q = \delta \left[\frac{P_d}{P_m} \right]_L^{\phi} Y_d^{\theta} \tag{5}$$

1. Note that equation 3 should not be interpreted to mean that the export price of the foreign country is P_f. The price charged domestically in the foreign country is P_f, in the currency of that country. A wedge develops between P_f and the country's export price (expressed in its currency) when the exchange rate changes and pass-through is incomplete. This phenomenon is captured by $|\rho| < 1$, not by any induced change in P_f (i.e., $\partial P_f/\partial R = 0$).

In equation 4, export volume responds to the export price as translated into foreign currency (P_xR), relative to the price of the competing good in the foreign market (P_f). The exponent β (< 0) is the price elasticity of foreign export demand. Similarly, export volume responds to the level of real GDP abroad (Y_f), with the exponent γ (>0) as the elasticity of exports with respect to real foreign income.

In equation 5, the real volume of imports responds to the ratio of domestic prices to import prices (in domestic currency). The price elasticity of imports is ϕ (> 0), which is positively signed in this specification because the domestic price is placed in the numerator and the import price in the denominator. The elasticity of imports with respect to domestic income is θ (> 0).

Equations 4 and 5 implicitly assume that it is a close approximation of reality to treat the supply of both exports and imports as "infinitely elastic" with respect to price. Otherwise it would be necessary to consider the interaction of both the supply and demand curves, using simultaneous-equation estimation methods. If supply is infinitely elastic, then changes observed in quantities imported or exported in response to changes in price will trace out movements along the demand curves for imports and exports, and statistical coefficients will represent demand price elasticities. As discussed in technical note 1 of the appendix, infinitely elastic supply of imports and exports should be a reasonable assumption for both the United States and Japan.

If data series on domestic prices, foreign prices, export prices, and import prices were readily available, it would be possible to directly estimate the trade volume equations 4 and 5. Then, in a second stage, import and export prices could be estimated as functions of the exchange rate and other variables. The estimated import and export prices could then be multiplied by the corresponding estimated trade quantities to obtain the trade values (e.g., as in Hooper and Marquez 1995).

However, the spirit of the Reduced Form Model (RFM) developed here is one of emphasis on data parsimony and ease of availability in data requirements. Whereas published data on import and export values are readily available, data permitting their decomposition into quantities and prices are less so, and it is often unclear whether the series available are strictly consistent.[2] The RFM deals with this problem by working directly

2. For the United States, for example, the IMF's *International Financial Statistics* reports only a "unit value" price series for exports and imports. These series are not only subject to the normal problems of unit value measures, but also are for aggregate trade, whereas the analysis here excludes oil. Import price series in particular will be heavily influenced by oil prices. The *Survey of Current Business* does report a series on nonoil import prices. However, as developed below, it turns out to be important to separate trade with industrial countries from that with developing countries, and there is no such separation in these price data. Moreover, if direct trade-price series for imports and exports are applied in the analysis, it then becomes necessary to add equations that can predict the trade prices (for example, as a function of exchange rates and other influences such as commodity

with the ratio of import and export values, rather than attempting to identify applicable import and export price series. Instead, as developed below, the key price variable is the real exchange rate between domestic and foreign prices. The equations that follow show first how the trade volume equations can be transformed into the trade value ratio and then how the trade prices can be mapped from the available real and nominal exchange rate series.

The first step is to obtain trade values as the product of trade volumes and (unmeasured) trade prices:

$$\begin{aligned} X^v &= X^q P_x \\ &= X^q P_d R^{\epsilon} \\ &= \alpha \left[\frac{P_x R}{P_f}\right]_L^{\beta} Y_f^{\gamma} P_d R^{\epsilon} \end{aligned} \tag{6}$$

$$\begin{aligned} M^v &= M^q P_m \\ &= M^q P_f R^{\rho} \\ &= \delta \left[\frac{P_d}{P_m}\right]_L^{\phi} Y_d^{\theta} P_f R^{\rho} \end{aligned} \tag{7}$$

In equation 6, export value (X^v) equals export volume (X^q) multiplied by export price (P_x). Substituting equation 2 for export price to take account of pass-through yields the second line in equation 6. The third line of the equation substitutes equation 4 for the components of export volume. Similarly, equation 7 substitutes equation 3 for import price and equation 5 for import volume to obtain the final expression for import value.

The ratio of import value to export value, the central dependent variable in this analysis, is then obtained in equation 8 by dividing equation 6 into equation 7. Taking the natural logarithm of both sides of 8 yields equation 9, which would be the estimating equation form if there were direct information on trade prices (P_x and P_m).

$$\frac{M^v}{X^v} = \frac{\delta}{\alpha} \frac{\left[\frac{P_d}{P_m}\right]_L^{\phi} Y_d^{\theta} P_f R^{\rho}}{\left[\frac{P_x R}{P_f}\right]_L^{\beta} Y_f^{\gamma} P_d R^{\epsilon}} \tag{8}$$

$$\begin{aligned} \ln\frac{M^v}{X^v} = \ln\frac{\delta}{\alpha} + \phi\ln\left[\frac{P_d}{P_m}\right]_L - \beta\ln\left[\frac{P_x R}{P_f}\right]_L + \theta\ln Y_d - \gamma\ln Y_f + \ln\frac{P_f}{P_d} \\ + (\rho - \epsilon)\ln R \end{aligned} \tag{9}$$

---

prices). The method here collapses this two-stage process through the use of the real exchange rate directly in the trade ratio equation.

Because equation 9 is in logarithmic form, the linear coefficients are elasticities. The equation shows that the percentage change in the ratio of import value to export value will equal the elasticity ϕ times the percentage change in the ratio of the domestic price to import price, minus the elasticity β times the percentage change in the ratio of the export price to the foreign price (both in foreign currency), plus the income elasticity θ times the percentage change in domestic income, minus the income elasticity γ times the percentage change in foreign income.

So far, the terms are the familiar price and income elasticities. However, there are two additional terms. The penultimate term shows the percentage change in the foreign price (in foreign currency) relative to the domestic price (in domestic currency). Thus, if inflation abroad is 3 percent and inflation domestically is 2 percent, other things being equal, the ratio of import value to export value will rise by the difference, or 1 percent. Note that this price term is contemporaneous and is part of the information on current trade prices (as opposed to the lagged trade prices that drive the trade volumes). The final term incorporates the influence of "pricing to market" or adopting less than complete pass-through, and depends on the change in the nominal exchange rate multiplied by the difference of the import and export pass-through coefficients. If pass-through is complete, $\epsilon = 0$ and $\rho = -1$. In that case, the last two terms in the equation can be consolidated into: $\ln [(P_f/R)/P_d]$, so that the percentage change in the ratio of import value to export value directly incorporates the percentage change in the foreign price (translated across the exchange rate with full pass-through) relative to the domestic price. Note further that it is the final term in equation 9 that gives rise to the "J-curve." Namely, if the currency depreciates in the current period, R declines, and $(\rho-\epsilon)R$ rises, pushing up the value of imports and therefore the import/export value ratio so long as the quantum of imports is still responding to the earlier (lagged) price variables.[3]

The final step in reaching the estimating equation is to make proper reformulations that permit use of the real exchange rate variable as the data input rather than (unobserved) import and export prices. The International Monetary Fund (1994b, 1995a) reports the real effective exchange rate (REER) for each country. In the country pages of this publication, the concept used is the ratio of domestic unit-labor cost in manufacturing to trade-weighted unit-labor costs in manufacturing in 20 industrial country trading partners. This measure may be designated as $R^* = (P_d/P_f)R$, in terms of the variables used so far. We then wish to reformulate equation 9 in terms that employ the real exchange rate, R^*.

As discussed below, the IMF's REER is an appropriate real exchange rate measure only for trade with the industrial countries. The strategy

3. This will be the normal outcome given the likely magnitudes of the parameters. Thus, a reasonable range for ρ is, say, -0.5 to -1; and a reasonable range for ϵ is 0 to -0.4; so $(\rho-\epsilon)$ will usually be negative, and its product with a negative change in R will be positive.

used in this study is to divide US trade in goods and nonfactor services into transactions with the industrial countries, on the one hand, and with the developing countries, on the other. For the latter, an alternative real exchange rate index based on the Dallas Federal Reserve estimates is applied. For purposes of the initial analytical exposition, however, it is helpful merely to refer to a general, overall real exchange rate.

Before proceeding with the development of the estimation model, however, it is important to consider why it is desirable, at least for the US case, to divide the model into trade with developed countries (DCs) and developing, or less developed, countries (LDCs). As will be shown below, the trends in the real exchange rate of the dollar have differed sharply between the two groups. There has been a long-term real appreciation of the dollar against LDC exchange rates but a secular depreciation of the real dollar against DC currencies. This fact alone would suggest possible benefits of disaggregating trade into the two groups, because if there were any differences in responsiveness to the real exchange rate between the two, aggregation could lead to severe distortions.[4]

A more fundamental reason why disaggregation of US trade into DC and LDC components may be revealing is that there have been major differences in secular trends for the two groups over the past two decades. Trade with such developing countries as the East Asian "Gang of Four"—South Korea, Taiwan, Hong Kong and Singapore—and more recently Mexico and China has shown rapid, outward-shifting supply of exports from these LDCs. As discussed at length below, this phenomenon (and its earlier precedent in trade with Japan) may have been responsible for the tendency of statistical studies to find higher income elasticities of demand for US imports than for US exports—the so-called Houthakker-Magee (1969) asymmetry. This asymmetry may have been a false attribution to differing demand functions of the impact of what in fact was caused by secular supply shifts (as discussed below). If so, then disaggregation into DC and LDC trade might help remove such a bias.[5]

Largely because there is no readily available real exchange rate index for Japanese trade with developing countries, the models developed below

4. For example, suppose the effective elasticity of the import/export value ratio with respect to the real exchange rate is unity for trade with DCs but 2 for trade with LDCs. Suppose the real rate against LDCs (r^*) rises by 10 percent, but the real rate against DCs (R^*) falls by 10 percent. If the value of trade with the two areas is approximately equal, an aggregate model will predict no change in trade, because the average real exchange rate has not changed. In contrast, the disaggregated model will show a rise in the import/export ratio for trade with LDCs that is twice as large as the decline in the corresponding ratio for trade with DCs, causing an overall rise in the import/export ratio.

5. Thus, Marquez (1993, 193) found that when US imports were disaggregated into trade with Canada, Japan, Germany, and the rest of world, and when the income elasticity was allowed to vary over time, "asymmetries in income elasticities for US trade were quite important until the mid-1970s but have virtually vanished since then."

do not similarly disaggregate trade for Japan. However, because the literature has not tended to show a major asymmetry in income elasticities for Japan's trade, disaggregation to deal with secular supply shifts from developing countries is presumably less important than in the US case.[6]

Returning to the analytical development of the estimating equations, it is necessary to restate the trade-ratio equations 8 and 9 in terms of the real exchange rate, for which data are available, rather than direct import and export prices, for which data are not (or at least not as readily) available. Consider first the import side. Here the price variable in the import quantity equation is: P_d/P_m. Equations 10 through 12 manipulate the definition of P_m (from equation 3) and R^* (just stated) to obtain a transformation of R* that is equivalent to P_d/P_m. This transformation is the ratio of the real exchange rate to the nominal exchange rate raised to unity plus the pass-through coefficient ρ (equation 12). Note that when pass-through is complete, the relationship is simply that the ratio P_d/P_m is equal to R^* (that is, the exponent on R in the right-hand denominator becomes zero, and the denominator becomes unity). In other words, when pass-through is complete, the ratio of domestic price to import price (both in domestic currency) is synonymous with the real exchange rate.

$$\frac{P_d}{P_m} = \frac{P_d}{P_f R^\rho} \tag{10}$$

$$R^* = \left[\frac{P_d}{P_f}\right] R = \left[\frac{P_d}{P_f R^\rho}\right] R^{1+\rho} = \frac{P_d}{P_m} R^{1+\rho} \tag{11}$$

$$\frac{P_d}{P_m} = \frac{R^*}{R^{1+\rho}} \tag{12}$$

Similarly, equation 13 shows the transformation that permits substituting the real exchange rate for the relative export price variable that drives export quantity. The left-hand side shows this price variable (the same as in equation 4). The first right-hand side expression substitutes equation 2, and the final right-hand side expression converts the result into a term using the real exchange rate R^*.

$$\frac{P_x R}{P_f} = \frac{P_d R^\epsilon R}{P_f} = R^* R^\epsilon \tag{13}$$

Once again, when pass-through is complete, so that $\epsilon = 0$, the relevant real export price becomes synonymous with the real exchange rate (because the final term R^ϵ turns into unity).

---

6. Thus, Hooper and Marquez (1995) find that for Japan over 1976–92 the import and export income elasticities are both close to unity.

Substituting equations 12 and 13 into 9, and moving the penultimate term in 9 to the left-hand side, we have:

$$\ln\frac{M^v}{X^v}-\ln\frac{P_f}{P_d}=\ln\frac{\delta}{\alpha}+\phi\ln\left[\frac{R^*}{R^{1+\rho}}\right]_L-\beta\ln[R^*R^\epsilon]_L+\theta\ln Y_d-\gamma\ln Y_f \quad (14)$$
$$+(\rho-\epsilon)\ln R$$

If we take as a close approximation that the lag operator of a sequence of ratios may be expressed as the lag operator on the sequence of numerators divided by the same lag operator on the sequence of denominators, then we may consider $[R^*/(R^{1+\rho})]_L \approx R^*_L/(R^{1+\rho})_L$, so that $\ln[R^*/(R^{1+\rho})]_L = \ln R^*_L - (1+\rho)\ln R_L$.[7] Similarly, $\ln[R^*R^\epsilon]_L \approx \ln R^*_L + \epsilon\ln R_L$. Rewriting equation 14 with this breakdown, and collecting terms, we have:

$$\ln\frac{M^v}{X^v}-ln\frac{P_f}{P_d}=\ln\frac{\delta}{\alpha}+(\phi-\beta)\ \ln R^*_L-[\phi(1+\rho)+\beta\epsilon]\ \ln R_L \quad (15)$$
$$+\theta\ln Y_d-\gamma\ln Y_f+(\rho-\epsilon)\ln R$$

Because quarterly data are to be employed, and there are seasonal variations, it is appropriate to add quarterly dummy variables, represented by D_i. The resulting final estimating equation is then:

$$\ln\frac{M^v}{X^v}-\ln\frac{P_f}{P_d}=\pi_0+\pi_1\ln R^*_L+\pi_2\ln R_L+\pi_3\ln Y_d+\pi_4\ln Y_f+\pi_5\ln R+\pi_iD_i;$$
$$\pi_1=\phi-\beta;$$
$$\pi_2=-[\phi(1+\rho)+\beta\epsilon]; \quad (16)$$
$$\pi_3=\theta;$$
$$\pi_4=-\gamma;$$
$$\pi_5=\rho-\epsilon$$

When this model is applied to trade with the developing countries, it confronts the problem that nominal exchange rates may not mean much, especially for Latin American countries, where inflation rates can reach several hundred percent. Fortunately, it is also in the developing countries where pass-through is likely to be close to complete. Developing country

7. Consider a simple lag operator of 0.6 weight on the current quarter and 0.4 weight on the previous quarter. Then the question is whether: $0.6R^*_t/R^{1+\rho}_t + 0.4R^*_{t-1}/R^{1+\rho}_{t-1} = [0.6R^*_t+0.4R^*_{t-1}]/[0.6R^{1+\rho}_t+0.4R^{1+\rho}_{t-1}]$. The latter equals: $0.6R^*_t/[0.6R^{1+\rho}_t+0.4R^{1+\rho}_{t-1}] + 0.4R^*_{t-1}/[0.6R^{1+\rho}_t+0.4R^{1+\rho}_{t-1}]$. When the variation in the nominal exchange rate from one quarter to the next is small, the approximation should be close. In the extreme case where $R_t = R_{t-1}$, the final right-hand side just indicated may be rewritten as: $0.6R^*_t/R^{1+\rho}_t + 0.4R^*_{t-1}/R^{1+\rho}_{t-1}$, confirming equality with the left-hand side.

For the eight-quarter lag operator actually used, the two highest weights are for the two adjacent middle quarters. Because the nominal exchange rates in adjacent quarters are likely to be similar, the approximation here should not be a severe distortion.

exporters and importers are likely to be "price takers" in the world market, rather than altering profit margins to partially offset price changes caused by exchange rate changes.

If pass-through is complete, so that $\epsilon = 0$ and $\rho = -1$, then the coefficient on the lagged nominal exchange rate in equation 15 collapses to zero, and the coefficient on the current nominal exchange rate collapses to minus unity. Using lowercase r to denote the relevant real exchange rate for trade with developing countries, equation 15 then transforms to:

$$\ln\frac{M^v}{X^v} - \ln\frac{P_f}{P_d} = \ln\frac{\delta}{\alpha} + (\phi - \beta)\ln r^*_L + \theta\ln Y_d - \gamma\ln Y_f - \ln r \qquad (17)$$

Shifting the last right-hand-side term to the left side, inverting the ratio P_f/P_d and correspondingly switching the sign of its logarithm, and consolidating the resulting left-side terms in light of the definition of the real exchange rate (equation 1), we have:

$$\ln\frac{M^v}{X^v} + \ln r^* = \ln\frac{\delta}{\alpha} + (\phi - \beta)\ln r^*_L + \theta\ln Y_d - \gamma\ln Y_f \qquad (18)$$

The estimating equation for US trade with developing countries thus becomes:

$$\ln\frac{M^v}{X^v} + \ln r^* = \lambda_0 + \lambda_1\ln r^*_L + \lambda_2\ln Y_d + \lambda_3\ln Y_f; \qquad (19)$$

$$\lambda_1 = \phi - \beta;$$
$$\lambda_2 = \theta;$$
$$\lambda_3 = \gamma$$

Finally, the model strategy of dividing trade into two blocs driven by two separate real exchange rates confronts the problem of omitting cross-price effects. Thus, the ratio of US imports from developing countries to US exports to developing countries will be affected not only by the direct price effect captured by the LDC real exchange rate, but also by the competitiveness of US goods against other industrial country goods in the LDC market, which in turn will depend on the DC real exchange rate against the dollar. To capture this substitution effect, it is possible to simply add the logarithm of the LDC real exchange rate lagged (r^*_L) to the right-hand side of the industrial country trade equation (16).[8] Similarly,

8. Formally, let P_x' be the price of US exports to LDCs (in dollars). Let P_{RW} be the price of LDC goods, expressed in dollars. If we assume US exporters do not feel compelled to reduce profit margins in sales to LDCs when the dollar appreciates, and more generally that pass-through is complete in trade with LDCs, then $P_x' = P_d$. Incorporation of the cross-price effect into the equations for trade with industrial countries will mean multiplying the right-hand side of equation 4 by the term: $[P_x'/P_{RW}]_L^{\Omega}$, where the parameter Ω reflects the degree of substitutability between LDC goods and US goods in DC markets; and multiplying the right-hand side of equation 5 by the term: $[P_d/P_{RW}]_L^{\psi}$, where the parameter ψ reflects substitutability between industrial and developing country goods in the US market. Defining $r^* = P_d/P_{RW}$, and under the assumption that $P_x' = P_d$, and following the steps of equations 6–13, the resulting change to equation 14) will be to add to the right-hand side the term:

the logarithm of the DC real exchange rate lagged (R^*_L) is added onto the right-hand side of the developing country trade equation (19).

Data Base

For the United States, the first step in estimation is to divide the data into trade with industrial and developing countries. Quarterly data on aggregate US nonoil imports of goods and nonfactor services (IMF, *International Financial Statistics*) are divided between industrial and developing countries on a basis of the respective shares in annual US merchandise imports (IMF, *Direction of Trade Statistics*).[9] It is assumed that trade in nonfactor services has the same proportional division between industrial and developing countries as merchandise trade. The same method is used to divide trade in goods and services on the side of US exports.

Next, it is necessary to obtain a real exchange rate index for US trade with developing countries (r^*). The Dallas Federal Reserve provides real exchange rate indexes for the dollar with respect to the currencies of Mexico, the rest of Western Hemisphere LDCs, Pacific newly industrializing countries (NICs), and other developing countries. A weighted average of these indexes is obtained on the basis of the shares of these areas in nonoil trade turnover with the United States in 1987.[10] For trade with industrial countries, the real exchange rate (R^*) selected is the IMF's REER deflated by unit-value labor costs in manufacturing (among 21 countries).

Figure 3 shows the path of the two real exchange rate indexes for the United States. Although both series show a sharp rise in the dollar from the late 1970s through the mid-1980s and then a decline, there are several major differences between the two.

First, the dollar did not rise as much against the LDC currencies as against DC currencies, though in part because the dollar had not fallen as much against the former from 1976 to 1978. Second, the peak of the real dollar occurred in early 1985 against DC currencies, but did not arrive until the first quarter of 1987 against the LDC currencies.[11] Third, the decline of the real dollar in the late 1980s was much more limited against the LDC currencies than against the DC currencies. Fourth, whereas the

---

$(\psi - \Omega)\ln r^*_L$. The corresponding estimation form in equation 16 adds to the right-hand side the term: $\pi_6 \ln r^*_L$, where $\pi_6 = \psi - \Omega$.

9. The aggregate nonoil import data deduct oil import series from CEA (1995). To calculate the DC-LDC shares, it is assumed that all imports from industrial countries are nonoil. Oil imports from developing countries are approximated as the amount of total imports from oil-exporting developing countries (IMF 1994c).

10. The weights are Mexico, 0.139; other Latin America, 0.218; Pacific NICs, 0.482; and other LDC, 0.161.

11. The collapse of the Mexican peso in 1986 in association with the oil price decline is one reason for this delay.

Figure 3 United States real effective exchange rates: developed versus less developed countries[a], 1976–second quarter 1995

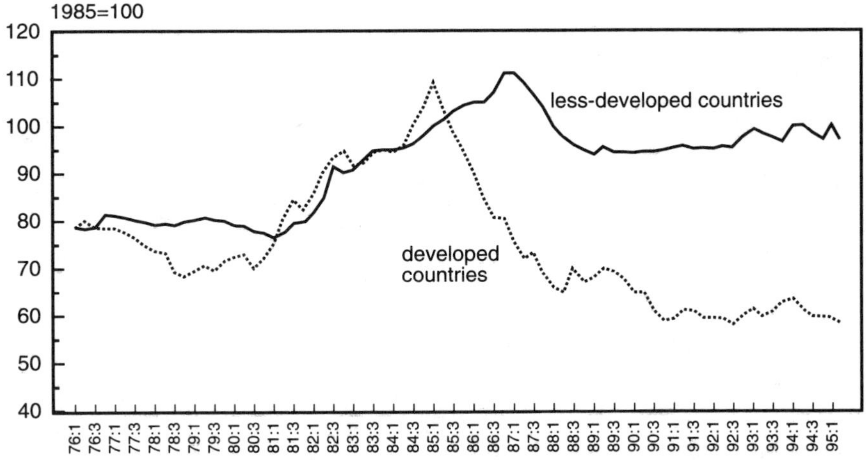

Sources: For developed-country series, IMF, *International Financial Statistics;* for developing-country series, the Dallas Federal Reserve.

a. Developed-country data deflated by unit-value labor costs and developing-country data by the consumer price index.

real dollar was considerably lower by the early 1990s than in the late 1970s against the industrial country currencies, the reverse was true for the dollar against LDC currencies. On this basis there has been a secular real appreciation of the dollar against LDC currencies, contrary to the general perception of secular decline of the dollar—which turns out to hold true only against DC currencies.[12] Fifth, the substantial drop of the dollar from early 1994 to the second quarter of 1995 is evident in the industrial country REER but is absent in the LDC measure.[13] Whereas there was some initial decline in late 1994 even against the LDC currencies, by early 1995 this drop had been reversed because of the sharp rise of the dollar against the Mexican peso, which offset the decline against Pacific NIC currencies.[14]

12. The pattern of rising relative purchasing-power-parity exchange rates as per capita income rises—attributable to the relative increase in the price of labor-intensive nontradeables (services) versus exchange rate determination in the tradables sector—would instead lead one to expect the opposite: secular real depreciation of the US dollar against LDC currencies when deflated by consumer prices (as in the Dallas Fed data).

13. The dollar rose against the peso from a real index of 86.6 in November to 149 by March but fell back to 127.2 by April—accounting for the modest dip in the LDC index from 1995:1 to 1995:2.

14. Note that the bulk of the analysis of this study considers the effect of the decline of the dollar through the second quarter of 1995. In August 1995 the dollar recovered much of this loss. The implications of the possibility that this recovery was permanent rather than transitory are discussed in chapter 4.

Figure 4 Japanese real effective exchange rate, 1978–second quarter 1995

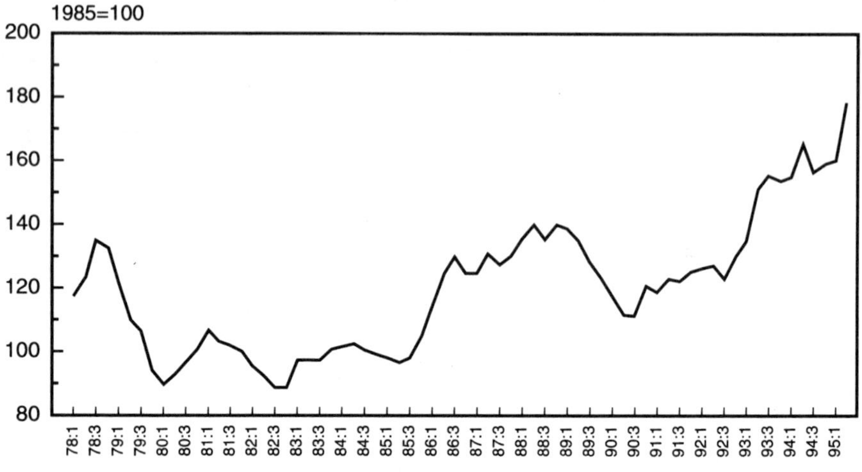

Source: IMF, *International Financial Statistics.*

The regional components of the Dallas Fed index are also revealing. From the fourth quarter of 1990 to that of 1994, the US currency was up by 11.6 percent in real terms against the currencies of the Pacific NICs. The dollar was down 20 percent in real terms against Latin American currencies (excluding the Mexican peso), reflecting the recovery of capital inflows to this region after the debt crisis. Against other regions excluding Europe and Japan, the real dollar was up by 9 percent between the two periods.

As discussed further below, the central point that emerges from separate consideration of LDC currencies is that in the 1990s the dollar has been stronger on an overall trade-weighted basis than on the basis of the IMF's REER, which considers only industrial countries, and this pattern has continued through 1994 and early 1995. The implication is that not as much reduction (after the usual time lag) is likely to be in store for the US deficit as might be expected on the basis of the substantial decline of the dollar against the industrial country currencies (especially the yen and mark) in early 1995.

Figure 4 shows the IMF's REER for Japan. The series shows a major decline from 1978 to the period 1980–85, associated with the 1979–80 oil price shock and, by 1984–85, with the unusual strength of the US dollar. The yen then rose sharply in real value during 1986–88. If the currency had stayed at its strong level of this period, it is likely that Japan's external accounts would have remained much closer to the modest surplus of 1990 (Cline 1994, chapter 4). However, a loose monetary policy associated with the early phase of the bubble economy in the late 1980s brought a phase of a weak yen in 1989–91, before the more recent strong-yen period of 1993 and after.

For the past two decades, the broad trend is toward a secular real appreciation of the yen against the other industrial country currencies. One reason for this trend has been the secular decline in real oil prices over this period. In 1980 Japan devoted two-fifths of its exports of goods and nonfactor services to imports of oil, whereas by the late 1980s the share was down to one-tenth (Cline 1994, chapter 4). A given external balance could thus be maintained with a more appreciated exchange rate in real terms. By the early 1990s, an additional factor explaining the strong yen was the ballooning current account surplus, driven in large part by weak import demand associated with the worst recession in the postwar period.[15]

Despite the secular rise of the yen, the currency has not risen as much as popular lore suggests. Thus, from 1978 to 1994 the REER for the yen rose by only 27 percent, an average rate of 1.5 percent per year. Even against the trough of 1980, the increase through 1994 was only 68 percent (IMF 1994b, 1995a). In contrast, commentators frequently cite the much larger nominal increase of the yen against the dollar—for example, a rise of 122 percent from 1980 (at 227 per dollar) to 1994 (at 102). The more moderate rise of the real, trade-weighted yen is partly attributable to much less inflation in Japan than in the United States over the period. From 1980 to 1994, wholesale prices rose by 34 percent in the United States, but fell by 16 percent in Japan (IMF 1994b, 1995a).

Correspondingly, the popular image of Japan's trade surplus as being impervious to the exchange rate because of structural rigidities including protection (e.g., Prestowitz 1988, 19) is inaccurate. This is partly because the yen's real rise of 1½ percent per year has been much more moderate than recognized, as just shown. The other reason is simply that the record is quite clear that Japan's trade performance does respond to the real exchange rate. This is evident in figure 2 and it is evident in the sizable and statistically significant coefficient relating the import/export ratio to the real exchange rate, found in the estimation results discussed below. Indeed, Cline (1994, 92) shows that the adjustment in US trade with Japan in the late 1980s after the correction of the overvalued dollar was just as great as the adjustment of US trade with the European Union when properly measured by percentage changes in exports and imports (rather than the misleading absolute bilateral trade balance).

15. Under some circumstances, such as those of the United States in the mid-1980s, there can be just the opposite relationship: a strong economy bids up interest rates and the currency. In the case of Japan by 1993 and after, the weak domestic economy meant that firms and banks were bringing back capital from abroad to bolster weak domestic asset positions, so the *ex ante* gap between dollars earned by the large current account surplus and private capital outflows put upward pressure on the yen.

The model estimates apply quarterly observations from 1978 (1976 for the lagged real exchange rate) through 1993 (Japan) or 1994 (United States). The dependent variable is the logarithm of the ratio of nonoil import value to export value (M^v/X^v) for goods and nonfactor services. This ratio is expressed in percentage form. The term P_f/P_d, relevant only for the industrial-country trade equations, refers to an index of foreign (20 industrial country) unit value of labor cost in local currency relative to home unit value of labor cost (1990 = 100).[16]

For the lagged DC real exchange rate (R^*_L), lagged LDC real exchange rate (r^*_L), and the lagged nominal exchange rate index (R_L), the lag structure assigns symmetrical weights over the most recent eight quarters. This structure, also applied in the multicountry model developed in Cline (1989), was adopted based on the earlier work of Helkie and Hooper (1988).[17]

Estimation of the import/export ratio rather than of individual equations for imports and exports separately forces the adoption of the same lag structure for the influence of the price variable on both imports and exports. Fortunately, for the United States Hooper and Marquez (1995) also arrive at an eight-quarter lag span for both exports and imports, even though they estimate separate equations for each. In contrast, Noland (1989) has found that for Japan, the best lag structure is much longer for imports (an *average* of 9.3 quarters) than for exports (4.6 quarters).[18] Nonetheless, as discussed below, the accuracy of the model is already high, so further refinement of the lag structure might provide little benefit.

The domestic and foreign income variables (Y_d and Y_f) are indexes of real GDP, with 1985:1 = 100. For Japan, foreign income is an export-weighted index of real GDP in the European Union, the United States, and Canada (IMF 1987, 1994a). For the United States, foreign income of industrial countries is an export-weighted index of GDP in the European Union, Canada, and Japan. For US trade with LDCs, foreign GDP is obtained based on an average of growth rates for developing-country regions (IMF, *World Economic Outlook*) weighted by US exports. In all cases, weights are for 1987, the midpoint of the period examined.

---

16. The ratio P_f/P_d is constructed by dividing the IMF's REER (R^*) into the organization's corresponding index for nominal effective exchange rates, or NEER. That is, REER = $[P_d/P_f]R$ = $[P_d/P_f]$NEER; P_f/P_d = NEER/REER. Note that in the estimation equations the base for the REER is 1985 = 100. Note also that this base gives a slightly larger drop in the REER for the dollar from 1985 to 1990 than does the REER series rebased to 1990 = 100.

17. The quarterly weights, beginning with the first quarter before the current quarter and working backward, are .067, .117, .15, .167, .167, .15, .117, .067 (Cline 1989, 148).

18. Experimentation with the flexible Tsurumi-Schmidt gamma lag model used by Noland might well improve statistical performance even with the single trade-ratio formulation used here. However, it would somewhat complicate use of the RFM model by others, especially in any future reestimation.

Trade Ratio Estimation Results

Table 1 reports regression estimates of equation 16 for Japan and for US trade with industrial countries and of equation 19 for US trade with developing countries. The US equations include both the direct and the cross-price real exchange rate term (R^* and r^*).[19] As all of the ordinary least-squares regressions of these equations show serial correlation, the results reported here apply correction for autocorrelation using Cochrane-Orcutt first-order autoregression (AR1).[20] Dummy variables are included for the first three quarters to account for seasonal variation.

As shown in table 1, the degree of explanation adjusted for degrees of freedom ($\bar{R}^2$) is high in all of the equations. The Durbin-Watson (DW) statistics suggest that the AR1 correction is successful in removing serial correlation. The Box-Ljung "Q" statistic, more appropriate than Durbin-Watson when AR1 is used, is not statistically significant for the US equations, confirming that serial correlation has been successfully removed. The Q statistic is statistically significant for the Japan equation, suggesting some remaining problems of serial correlation despite the DW statistic of nearly 2 (the level of noncorrelation).[21]

The statistical significance of the individual parameters (t statistics are shown in parentheses) is generally high for trade with industrial countries (US) and for Japan's trade, with an important exception being the coefficient on foreign income in the trade ratio equation for Japan. In contrast, for US trade with developing countries, the coefficients on both domestic and foreign growth were implausible in size (and in one case, sign) and statistically insignificant. Accordingly, they are both constrained to equal unity in the estimates shown here.

In general, the estimated coefficients on real exchange rates are relatively high. The absolute sum of direct and cross-price import and export price elasticities ($\phi - \beta$ and $\psi - \Omega$, respectively) substantially exceeds unity, the critical threshold of the "Marshall-Lerner condition" for depre-

---

19. Note that for US trade with DCs, the regression parameter on ln R^*_L is $\phi - \beta$ and the parameter on ln r^*_L is $\psi - \Omega$, whereas for US trade with LDCs the reverse is true (because in this case r^* represents the direct price effect and R^* the cross-price effect).

20. Autoregressive structure is of the form: $\hat{y}_t = a(1-\text{rho}) + b(X_t - \text{rho}\cdot X_{t-1}) + \text{rho}\cdot y_{t-1}$.

21. Note further that a side benefit of using the ratio of imports to exports as the dependent variable is that the resulting time series is stationary. This might be guessed from figure 1. More formally, regressing the import/export ratio of period t on that for period $t-1$ and a constant yields a coefficient of 0.953 (with a standard error of 0.04). The Dickey-Fuller test statistic, which involves the difference of this coefficient from unity (as normalized by the ratio of the variance of: the dependent variable minus this coefficient times the lagged dependent variable; to the variance of the dependent variable; Harvey 1994, 131) is -5.3, compared with a critical threshold of -3.5 for significance at the 1 percent level. The unit-root hypothesis—that the series is a random walk with drift, rather than mean-reverting and stationary—is thus rejected.

Table 1 Regression results[a]

Dependent variable	Coefficient[b]										
Independent variable:	π_0 constant	π_1 $\ln R^*_L$	π_2 $\ln R_L$	π_3 $\ln Y_d$	π_4 $\ln Y_f$	π_5 $\ln R$	π_6 $\ln r^*_L$	RHO	$\bar{R}^2$	D.W.	Q
Analytical:	$\ln(\delta/\alpha)$	$\phi-\beta$ $(\psi-\Omega)$	$-[\phi(1+\rho)+\beta\epsilon]$	θ	$-\gamma$	$\rho-\epsilon$	$\psi-\Omega$ $(\phi-\beta)$				
United States											
A. Developed countries											
$\ln[M^v/X^v]-$	−6.682	0.827	−0.183	1.526	−1.379	0.033	0.709	0.502	0.960	1.93	22.2
$\ln[P_f/P_d]$	(8.7)	(2.0)	(.4)	(3.4)	(3.6)	(.3)	(3.0)	(4.7)			
B. Developing countries											
$\ln[M^v/X^v]$	0.634	0.816	...	1	−1	...	1.316	0.989	0.982	2.06	18.1
$+\ln r^*$	(0.2)	(2.9)	...	c	c	...	(2.2)	(44.6)			
Japan											
C. Total											
$\ln[M^v/X^v]-$	−3.42	1.989	−1.035	0.919	−0.994	−0.260	...	0.491	0.892	1.95	26.1
$\ln[P_f/P_d]$	(1.5)	(7.7)	(2.9)	(1.9)	(1.0)	(1.7)		(3.8)			

a. For Japan, Y_d is lagged one quarter.

b. *T* statistics are shown in parentheses.

c. Constrained.

ciation to improve the country's trade balance. The sum of elasticities is nearly 2 for Japan, and about 1.5 for the United States.

For the United States, in both the DC and LDC equations, the sum of direct price elasticities ($\phi - \beta$) is higher than the sum of cross-price elasticities ($\psi - \Omega$), as might be expected. Typically, the most important relative price for US trade with, say, France is that between US goods and French goods. However, the US equation for trade with industrial countries has a somewhat lower direct price elasticity, and higher cross-price elasticity relative to the magnitude of the direct elasticity, than might be expected. If valid, this result would indicate an important role for US competition with developing countries in the determination of US trade with industrial countries.[22] The US equation for trade with developing countries has the pattern of larger divergence between the direct and cross-price elasticities that might be expected, but also shows a high degree of cross-price effects (this time for US-DC competition in developing-country markets).

An important finding in table 1 is the result that the Houthakker-Magee asymmetry is absent. This effect refers to the usual finding that the income elasticity of US imports is considerably larger than that for exports (typically on the order of 2 and 1, respectively; see, e.g., Hooper and Marquez 1995). Instead, equation A places the US income elasticity for trade with industrial countries at 1.526, and the export income elasticity at 1.379, giving only a marginal difference.

There is an important economic reason why the method here might reject the Houthakker-Magee asymmetry. The most plausible explanation for this phenomenon has always been that it is a statistical artifact representing time trends rather than a meaningful difference in income elasticities. Namely, there could be a secular rise in US imports relative to exports caused by outward-shifting supply and catch-up in technology and product quality by newly industrializing countries (and in an earlier period, Japan). Because income rises over time, such shifts could be misattributed in regression analysis to a high income elasticity for imports.[23]

---

22. For example, between US agricultural exports and those from Latin America in other OECD markets, on the export side; and between footwear and apparel from Italy versus the East Asian four tigers, on the import side.

23. In principle, any such shifts are picked up in the relative price variables, attributing trade trends to changes in prices. However, the difficulties of incorporating quality and product changes into the indexes, and possible problems with price indexes in accurately reflecting even prices of unchanged goods in the face of outward-shifting foreign supply, mean that more rapid import than export growth for the United States may tend to be picked up instead in the form of asymmetric income elasticities. Note that Helkie and Hooper (1988) attempt to introduce a foreign capital-stock variable as a proxy to remove the influence of these shifts, and their method does remove the Houthakker-Magee asymmetry. However, subsequently Hooper and Marquez (1995) return to the more standard equation and obtain the asymmetry again. They note that if the purpose is projection, the difference is moot so long as the relative capital accumulation trends continue.

In estimates that separate out DC trade from LDC trade, as in equations A and B of table 1, it could thus make sense that the Houthakker-Magee asymmetry would disappear. It might be argued that the findings here do not constitute a robust rejection of the asymmetry, because the income elasticities for trade with LDCs are statistically insignificant and must be imposed by constraint rather than estimated directly. There are two responses to this possible critique. First, the finding of no asymmetry in trade with DCs (where the coefficients are estimated directly) would seem important in its own right. Second, because there is no underlying theory to the Houthakker-Magee asymmetry, the proper null hypothesis should be elasticity symmetry rather than asymmetry. Methodologically, the burden of proof should then be on the case for asymmetry. A statistically insignificant finding does not reject the null hypothesis of symmetry. On the contrary, it should require a statistically significant difference in the elasticities to confirm the Houthakker-Magee hypothesis.

This being said, there is the possibility of a bias in the estimates here in that they may be attributing trend factors to the real LDC exchange rate (r^*) rather than to differential income elasticities, as is more usually the case. As figure 3 shows, there is a long-term trend in the US real exchange rate against LDC currencies. The regressions show high coefficients on this real rate. There is thus a possibility that the true impact of the LDC real exchange rate is being overstated—especially in the coefficient on the cross-price term in the US-DC trade equation—whereas the influence of an adverse time trend in the US trade ratio (which would otherwise show up in asymmetric income elasticities) is being understated. In short, while the findings here provide an intriguing rejection of the usual Houthakker-Magee asymmetry, an important area for further research would be confirmation of this result in alternative tests similarly using disaggregated DC-LDC data.[24]

There is no income elasticity asymmetry in the results for Japan either, even though in this case there is no inclusion of an LDC real exchange rate in the equation. The estimates here place the elasticities at about unity on both the export and import sides. These findings are consistent with those of Hooper and Marquez (1995), who estimate Japan's income

24. Cline (1989) implicitly goes in this direction by estimating bilateral trade equations between pairs of "countries" with the world divided into 17 countries or groupings. The weighted average US income elasticities in that analysis are 2.44 for imports and 1.7 for exports, giving a somewhat smaller difference than frequently found (albeit not because there is a smaller difference for trade with DCs than with LDCs). However, the estimates here not only distinguish between industrial and developing countries, but also deal with the import/export ratio rather than with *levels* of imports and exports separately. Because data on trade levels are more subject to time trends, and because the underlying suspicion about the Houthakker-Magee effect is that it is basically a time trend, the approach here may have an additional reason for avoiding misattribution of such trends to income elasticity differentials.

Figure 5 United States: RFM backcasts of trade ratios for trade with developed countries

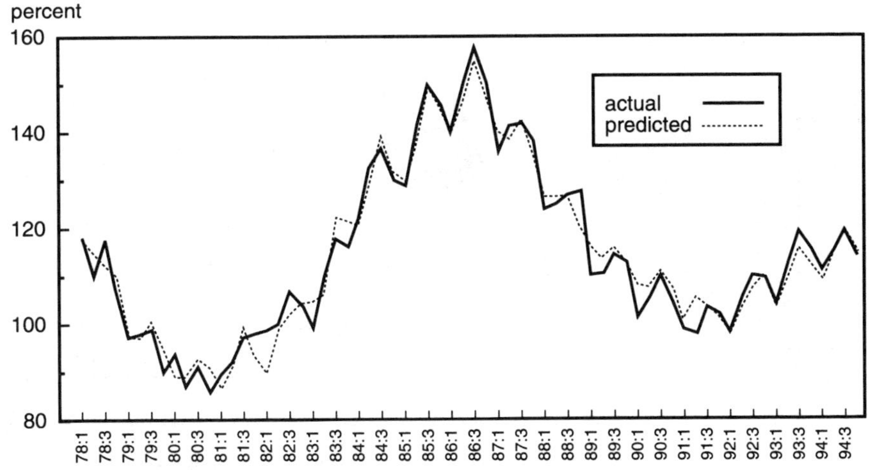

elasticities at unity for both imports and exports. This income neutrality of the Japanese equation is encouraging, because conversely a finding of higher export income elasticity than import income elasticity would have confirmed the view that a secular real appreciation of the yen is required just to maintain a constant ratio of exports to imports (e.g., Krugman 1991a, 10).

Finally, the coefficients of the lagged and current nominal exchange rate provide indirect information on the extent of price pass-through. There are two estimated parameters (π_2 and π_5), which represent four unknowns (ρ, ϵ, ϕ, and β). As discussed in technical note 2 of the appendix, the direct estimates of the coefficients π_2 and π_5 turn out generally to be inconsistent with plausible values for the underlying pass-through parameters. Nonetheless, the estimates are not significantly different from values that would be consistent with normal pass-through ratios.

More generally, the import/export ratio approach used in the model is not ideal for obtaining robust estimates of the pass-through ratios. There is the inherent problem that the equation can only identify values for combinations of the pass-through and price elasticities, not the specific values for each. The results suggest, additionally, that statistical significance of the pass-through estimates is weak. This outcome suggests that for purposes requiring more precise knowledge of the individual price elasticities and pass-through ratios, the more traditional approach of estimating separate import and export equations is more appropriate.

Figures 5 through 7 show the backcasts of the ratio of nonoil imports of goods and nonfactor services to exports of goods and nonfactor services for US trade with industrial countries, US trade with developing countries,

Figure 6 United States: RFM backcasts of trade ratios for trade with developing countries

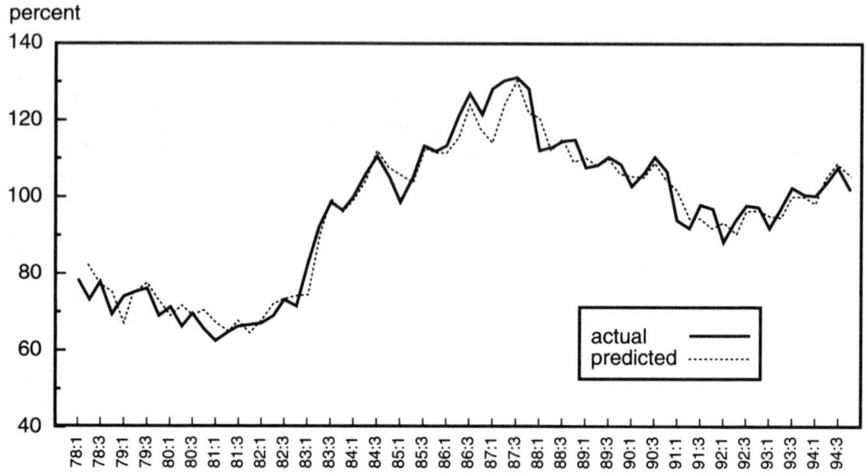

Figure 7 Japan: RFM backcasts of trade ratios

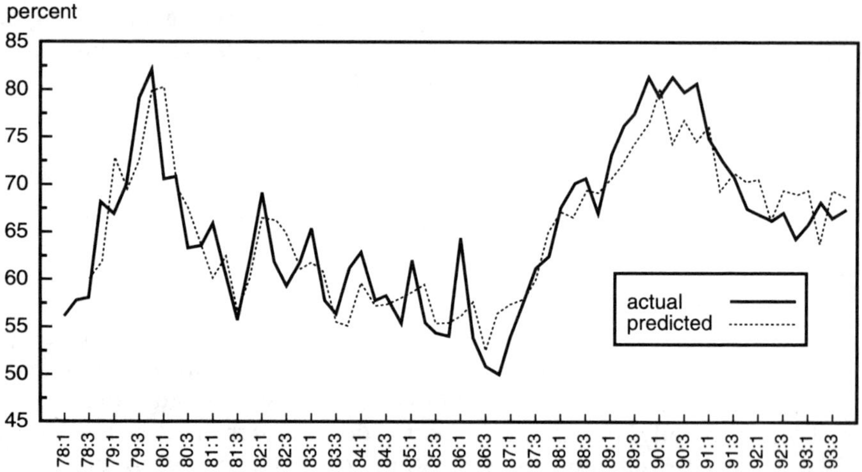

and Japanese total trade. The fit over the whole period is good for all three equations. These equations thus provide the basis for the current account projections developed below.

Factor Services and Transfers

With the trade ratio equations in hand, the next step in implementing the RFM is to add extremely simple linear time trends for the other elements

Figure 8 United States: exports of goods and nonfactor services to developed and developing countries, quarterly, 1978–94

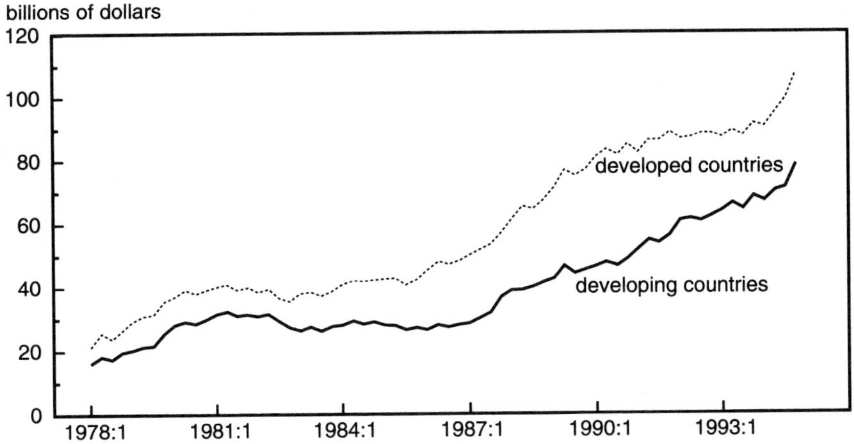

Sources: IMF, *International Financial Statistics; Direction of Trade Statistics.*

of the current account: net factor services and transfers. In addition, it is necessary to project the absolute level of exports of goods and nonfactor services in order to obtain the base to which the trade ratio can be applied. As for oil imports, there is no attempt to explain past series. For backcasting, the model simply incorporates the actual oil import value. For forecasting, the assumption made below is that nominal oil import values rise at a specified (2 percent nominal) rate, but other rules of thumb could be equally plausible.

Figure 8 shows the nominal dollar value of US exports of goods and nonfactor services to industrial and developing countries over the past 15 years.[25] There are clearly two periods: a phase of stagnation in 1980–86, when the dollar was strong, and a phase of rapid growth in 1987–94 after the decline of the dollar. Figure 8 also depicts the more severe stagnation of US exports to the developing countries during 1982–86, suggesting that the Latin American debt crisis also played a role, in addition to that of the overvalued dollar.

For Japan, figure 9 shows a trend for the dollar value of exports of goods and nonfactor services that is close to linear over almost the entire period. The linearity in both the US and Japanese export performance (with the adjustment for two phases in the case of the United States) is somewhat surprising. Normally one would anticipate geometric growth. However, these are nominal series, and falling inflation over this period

25. Note that these data are quarterly and should be multiplied by four to correspond with the levels reported in table 3.

Figure 9 Japan: exports of goods and nonfactor services, 1980–94

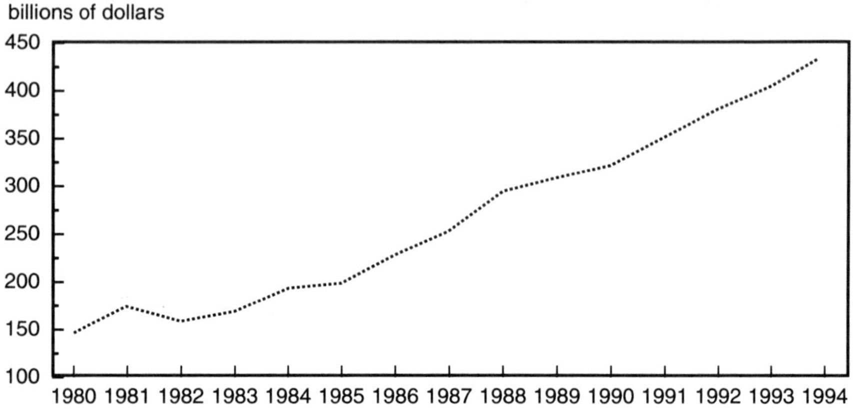

Source: IMF, *International Financial Statistics.*

tends to counter geometric volume increases and thus to yield linear trends.

Because estimation of goods and services exports is primarily for purposes of scaling the base to which the estimated import/export ratio can be applied, finesse is not essential. The barebones strategy of the model thus calls for application of linear trends, rather than a more complete modeling of the export base (e.g., directly incorporating exchange rates, growth, and other variables). The linear time trends used for this purpose are reported in table 2.

Factor (capital) services are the next component. Figure 10 shows the nominal levels of factor services income and payments for the United States and Japan. There is an evident narrowing of the gap between income and payments for the United States over time and a widening of that gap, especially by the early 1990s, for Japan. This is what one would expect to see because the United States has been a chronic deficit country since the early 1980s and Japan a chronic surplus country, and there should be a corresponding reduction in the historic US net earnings from its foreign assets and an increase in those of Japan. Indeed, the surprise so far has been that US net capital services remained positive long after the US net foreign asset position turned negative.

It is easy to expend enormous modeling effort in explaining capital services. Direct investment needs to be distinguished from portfolio investment. There are questions of book value versus market value for direct investment. Historically, rates of return on US direct investment abroad have been higher than returns on portfolio investment, and higher than rates of return on foreign direct investment in the United States. Portfolio rates of return tend to vary with interest rates. There are different rates of return on government versus private assets.

Table 2 Linear time trend equations

Concept	Period	Constant (billions of dollars)	Coefficient on time (billions of dollars)	t=1	Dummies
Exports of goods and nonfactor services ($\hat{X}$)					
US					
developed	1983–87	134.6	14.2	1983	•
	1987–94	215.6	22.8	1987	•
developing	1983–87	104.1	2.4	1983	•
	1987–94	101.0	23.5	1987	•
Japan	1983–94	135.8	24.4	1983	•
Net factor services ($\hat{F}$)					
US	1980–90	38.5	−1.5	1980	•
	1990–94	42.1	−7.5	1990	•
Japan	1980–94	−8.99	2.87	1980	•
Transfers ($\hat{T}$)					
US					
Private	1982–94	−7.80	−0.56	1982	•
Official	1980–94	−6.18	−0.86	1980	
					90: −4.96
					91: 37.1
Japan	1980–86	−0.85	−0.19	1980	•
	1987–94	−0.85	−0.19	1980	all: −1.8
					91: −7.6

Attempting to model these aspects would defeat the purpose of the RFM, which is to offer simplicity and facility in forecasting. Instead, the approach for factor services is once again to resort to a simple linear time trend. Figure 11 shows net factor services for the United States and Japan. Once again, there is a surprisingly steady linear nominal trend for Japan, upward. The downward trend for the United States is certainly present but shows much sharper fluctuations. Moreover, the US trend becomes much more precipitate after 1990.

Linear extrapolation of net factor services runs the risk of failing to capture acceleration in the downward trend resulting from interest payments coming due on new external debt accumulated from future annual current account deficits. The EAG model explicitly incorporates this cumulative process, which amounts to a reinforcing feedback mechanism in any long-term trend of external deficits (and conversely, reinforcement of surpluses for countries with chronic surpluses).

The linear equations for net factor services (table 2) adopt two periods: 1980–90 and 1990–94. In the forecasts discussed below, it is possible to

Figure 10 United States and Japan: factor services income and payments, 1980–93

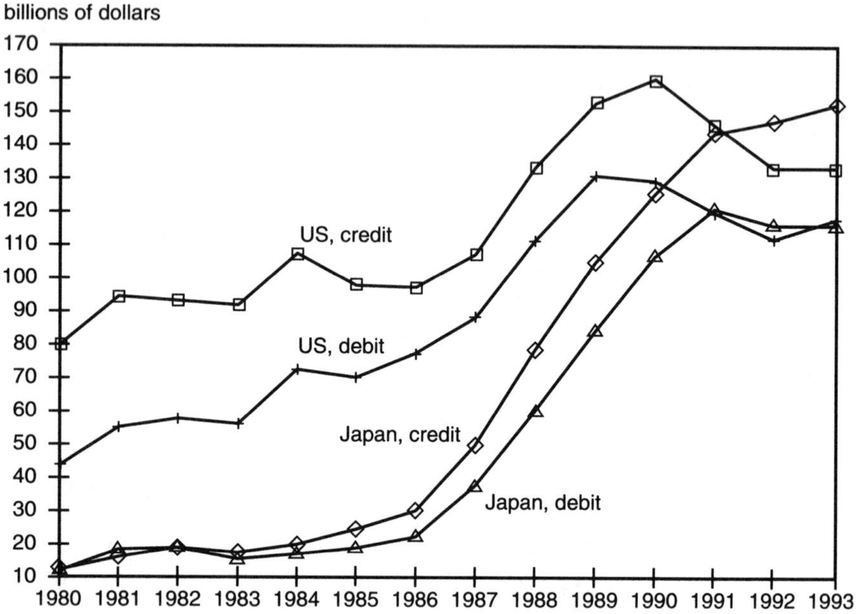

Figure 11 United States and Japan: net factor services, 1980–94

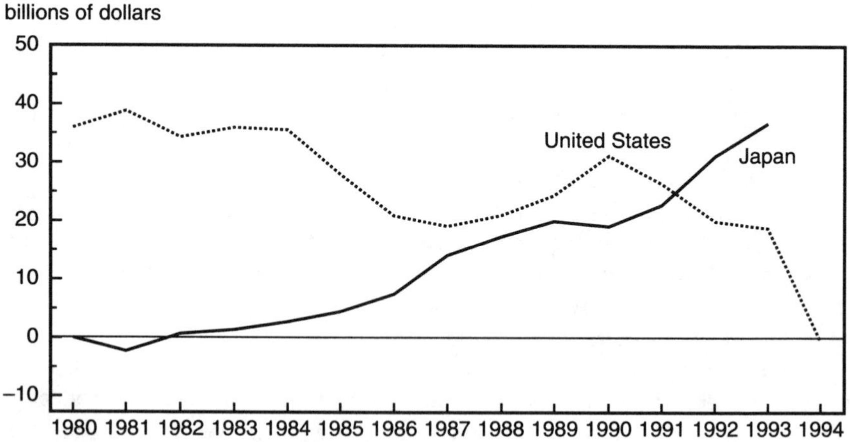

Source: IMF, *International Financial Statistics.*

use the EAG model projections of net factor services as a check on the simpler RFM extrapolations. As it turns out, the slope of the RFM linear trend line for 1990–94 is sufficiently steep that the change projected below

Figure 12 United States: net transfers, 1980–94

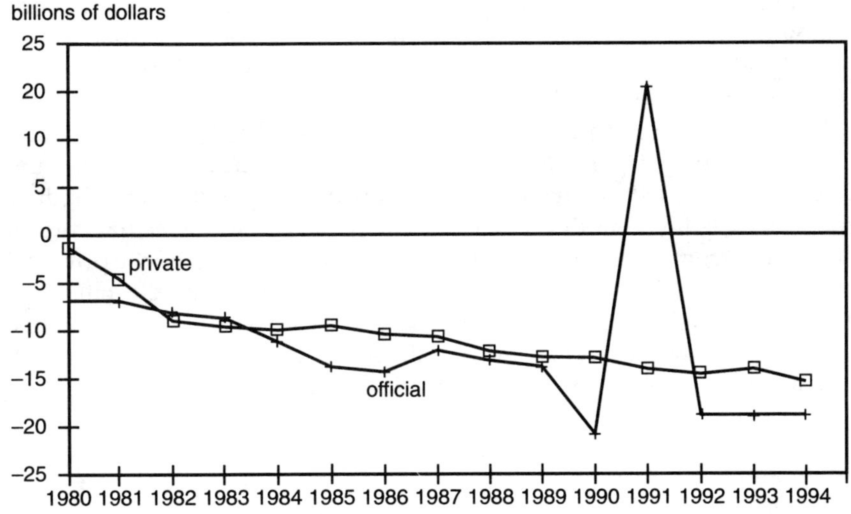

from 1994 to 1997 is close to that calculated with the more complete EAG model. Both show the US net factor services balance deteriorating in this period at a rate of about $7.5 billion per year.

The final component of the current account is net transfers. Figure 12 shows private and government transfers for the United States. Net official transfers grew from outflows of about $7 billion in the early 1980s to a plateau of about $18 billion by the early 1990s. The large shift to positive transfers in 1991 reflects payments received from allies for US efforts in the Gulf War, and the bulge in net negative transfers in 1990 may also have been associated with the war.[26] As reported in table 2, the trend line for official transfers incorporates dummy variables to remove these shifts.

Japan's net transfers have been modest and reached only about $5 billion annually by the early 1990s (with the exception of 1991 when there were large payments in connection with the Gulf War). Table 2 reports the time trend for these net transfers.

Current Account Model and Backcasts

The resulting overall model of the current account is:

$$CA_t = \hat{X}[1-\hat{Z}] - \hat{O} + \hat{F} + \hat{T} \qquad (20)$$

The initial export term $\hat{X}$ is exports of goods and nonfactor services (linear trend), and the term $\hat{Z}$ is the predicted ratio of nonoil imports of goods

26. The United States forgave half of Egypt's debt in 1990 in the context of the war. It also forgave half of US claims on Poland in that year, in support of the process of economic transition.

and nonfactor services to exports of goods and nonfactor services from the equations in table 1.[27] The product $\hat{X}[1-\hat{Z}]$ is the balance on goods and nonfactor services excluding oil. The current account estimate is then completed by subtracting oil imports ($\hat{O}$), and adding net factor services ($\hat{F}$) and net transfers ($\hat{T}$).[28]

Tables 3 and 4 report the resulting actual and RFM-predicted values for the various components of the US and Japanese current accounts, and figures 13 and 14 show the overall comparisons. As shown in the figures, the backcasts for 1983 through 1994 adhere closely to the actual current account outcomes, especially for the United States. For Japan, the principal divergence occurs in 1990, when the deficit fell to only $36 billion as against a model backcast of about $55 billion. Conceivably, a cumulative effect of the bubble economy (which, however, brought the highest growth rate as early as 1988) could have contributed to this result.

27. The direct estimates from the equations are quarterly, and must be converted to annual averages for the year in question for compatibility with the annual current account data in equation 20.

28. For the United States, the balance on trade on goods and services is estimated separately for industrial and developing countries. Thus:

$$CA_t = \hat{X}_{DC,t}[1-\hat{Z}_{DC,t}] + \hat{X}_{LDC,t}[1-\hat{Z}_{LDC,t}] - \hat{O}_t + \hat{F}_t + \hat{T}_t$$

Table 3 United States: actual and predicted current account, 1980-94 (billions of dollars)

	Exports of goods and nonfactor services				Imports of goods and nonfactor services					
Year	Goods	NFS	Actual XGS	Predicted XGS	Goods	Oil	Nonoil	NFS	Actual NOMGS	Predicted NOMGS
1980	224.3	40.4	264.7	—	249.8	79.5	170.3	40.3	210.5	—
1981	237.1	50.1	287.0	—	265.1	78.4	186.7	44.2	230.9	—
1982	211.2	58.4	269.6	—	247.7	62.0	185.7	50.2	235.9	—
1983	201.8	58.4	260.2	255.4	268.9	55.1	213.8	53.2	267.0	265.9
1984	219.9	65.0	284.9	272.0	332.4	58.1	274.3	65.7	340.0	327.8
1985	215.9	66.4	282.3	288.7	338.1	51.4	286.7	70.8	357.5	368.7
1986	223.4	78.3	301.6	305.4	368.4	34.3	334.1	77.7	411.8	413.9
1987	250.2	88.4	338.7	362.9	409.8	42.9	366.9	87.5	454.3	487.7
1988	320.2	98.8	419.0	409.2	447.2	39.6	407.6	94.3	501.9	494.4
1989	361.7	113.9	475.6	455.5	477.4	50.9	426.5	97.7	524.2	503.1
1990	388.7	132.0	520.7	501.8	497.6	62.3	435.3	112.4	547.6	535.0
1991	417.0	145.7	562.6	548.1	490.7	51.7	439.0	113.0	552.1	545.2
1992	440.1	159.4	599.5	594.4	536.3	51.6	484.7	117.1	601.8	593.7
1993	456.9	164.2	621.1	640.7	589.4	51.5	537.9	121.8	659.7	669.1
1994	502.7	172.3	675.0	687.0	669.1	51.2	617.9	128.0	745.9	755.9

Table 3 United States: actual and predicted current account, 1980-94 (billions of dollars) *(Continued)*

	Factor Services		Transfers		Current account		DC REER	LDC REER	Trade ratio[a] (percent)	
	Actual	Predicted	Actual	Predicted	Actual	Predicted	(1990 = 100)		Actual	Predicted
1980	36.0	—	−8.3	−14.9	2.2	—	125.0	83.5	79.5	—
1981	39.0	—	−11.7	−16.4	5.0	—	140.2	83.2	80.4	—
1982	33.9	—	−17.0	−17.9	−11.4	—	158.3	92.6	87.5	—
1983	36.0	32.5	−17.8	−19.4	−43.6	−52.5	161.9	98.9	102.6	104.1
1984	35.0	31.0	−20.6	−20.9	−98.8	−103.8	171.3	102.4	119.3	120.5
1985	27.7	29.5	−23.0	−22.4	−121.7	−124.3	174.0	109.0	126.6	127.7
1986	21.1	28.0	−24.1	−23.9	−147.5	−138.7	137.6	114.2	136.5	135.5
1987	18.2	26.5	−23.1	−25.4	−163.5	−166.6	117.1	114.0	134.2	134.4
1988	20.8	25.0	−25.0	−26.9	−128.3	−126.7	108.3	102.9	119.8	120.8
1989	23.9	23.5	−25.6	−28.4	−102.9	−103.4	110.3	100.1	110.2	110.5
1990	31.7	34.6	−33.0	−34.9	−91.7	−95.8	100.0	100.0	105.2	106.6
1991	26.3	27.1	6.6	5.7	−6.9	−16.0	96.2	101.7	98.1	99.5
1992	20.4	19.6	−32.9	−32.9	−67.9	−64.2	94.3	102.2	100.4	99.9
1993	18.3	12.1	−32.1	−34.4	−103.9	−102.2	98.5	103.7	106.2	104.4
1994	0.5	4.6	−34.1	−35.9	−155.7	−151.4	97.5	104.6	110.5	110.0

NFS = nonfactor services
XGS = exports of goods and nonfactor services
NOMGS = nonoil imports of goods and nonfactor services
REER = real effective exchange rate

a. Nonoil imports of goods and nonfactor services to exports of goods and nonfactor services.

Table 4 Japan: actual and predicted current account, 1980-94 (billions of dollars)

	Exports of goods and nonfactor services				Imports of goods and nonfactor services					
Year	Goods	NFS	Actual XGS	Predicted XGS	Goods	Oil	Nonoil	NFS	Actual NOMGS	Predicted NOMGS
1980	126.7	19.9	146.6	—	124.6	57.8	66.8	31.0	97.8	—
1981	149.5	23.4	172.9	—	129.6	58.7	70.9	34.9	105.8	—
1982	137.7	22.0	159.7	—	119.6	51.4	68.2	32.3	100.5	—
1983	145.5	21.2	166.7	160.2	114.0	45.7	68.3	31.9	100.2	93.0
1984	168.3	22.5	190.8	184.6	124.0	45.5	78.5	32.8	111.3	106.5
1985	174.0	22.5	196.5	209.0	118.0	40.6	77.4	32.7	110.1	119.2
1986	205.6	23.5	229.1	233.4	112.8	24.1	88.7	35.5	124.2	129.8
1987	224.6	28.8	253.4	257.8	128.2	27.5	100.7	48.4	149.1	154.3
1988	259.8	35.0	294.8	282.2	164.8	25.8	139.0	63.5	202.5	191.6
1989	269.6	39.7	309.3	306.6	192.7	29.8	162.9	75.0	237.9	223.8
1990	280.4	40.8	321.2	331.0	216.8	41.2	175.6	82.0	257.6	253.1
1991	306.6	44.6	351.2	355.4	203.5	37.8	165.7	85.0	250.7	254.7
1992	330.9	48.3	379.2	379.8	198.5	37.8	160.7	89.7	250.4	261.1
1993	351.3	51.5	402.8	404.2	209.7	33.1	176.6	92.8	269.4	272.6
1994	384.0	51.5	435.5	—	238.2	32.6	205.6	92.8	298.4	—

Table 4 Japan: actual and predicted current account, 1980-94 (billions of dollars) *(Continued)*

	Factor Services		Transfers		Current account		REER	Trade ratio[a] (percent)	
	Actual	Predicted	Actual	Predicted	Actual	Predicted	(90 = 100)	Actual	Predicted
1980	−0.2	−6.1	−1.5	−1.1	−10.8	—	82.9	66.7	69.5
1981	−2.1	−3.2	−1.6	−1.3	4.8	—	89.7	61.2	59.9
1982	0.4	−0.3	−1.4	−1.5	6.8	—	80.0	62.9	63.6
1983	1.6	2.6	−1.6	−1.7	20.8	22.5	85.1	60.1	58.0
1984	2.6	5.5	−1.5	−1.9	35.0	36.2	88.1	58.3	57.7
1985	5.1	8.4	−1.7	−2.0	49.2	55.5	87.5	56.0	57.0
1986	7.0	11.3	−2.1	−4.0	85.8	86.8	107.4	54.2	55.6
1987	13.8	14.2	−3.7	−4.2	87.0	86.0	111.9	58.8	59.9
1988	17.3	17.1	−4.1	−4.4	79.6	77.4	119.8	68.7	67.9
1989	19.7	20.0	−4.3	−4.6	57.0	68.4	113.7	76.9	73.0
1990	18.9	22.9	−5.5	−4.8	35.9	54.8	100.0	80.2	76.5
1991	22.7	25.8	−12.5	−10.8	72.9	77.9	105.9	71.4	71.7
1992	31.3	28.7	−4.6	−5.2	117.6	104.4	109.9	66.0	68.7
1993	37.3	31.6	−6.1	−5.4	131.5	124.7	129.0	66.9	67.4
1994	—	—	—	—	129.3	—	137.8	68.5	—

NFS = nonfactor services
XGS = Exports of goods and nonfactor services
NOMGS = Nonoil imports of goods and nonfactor services
REER = real effective exchange rate

Figure 13 United States: actual and predicted current account, 1983–94

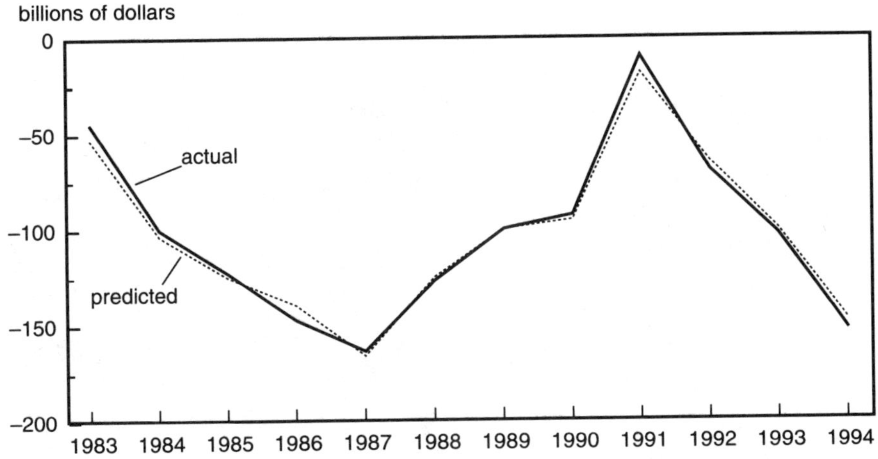

Sources: IMF, *International Financial Statistics* and RFM backcast.

Figure 14 Japan: actual and predicted current account, 1983–94

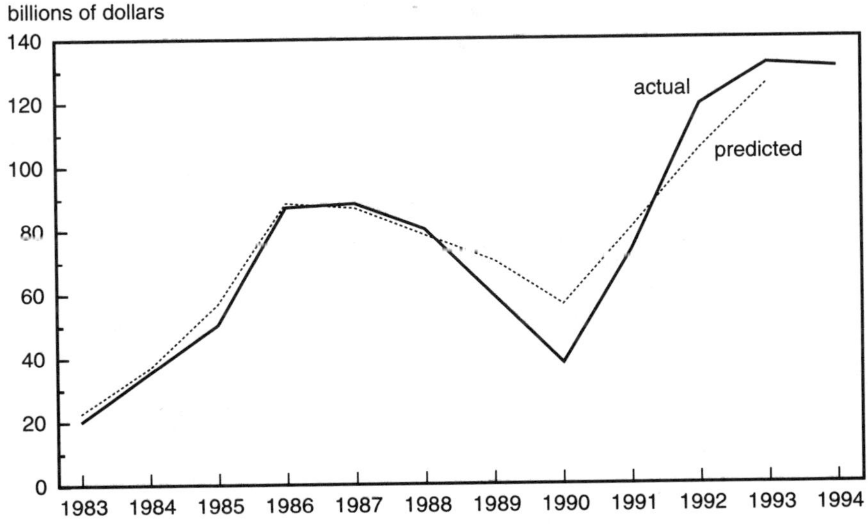

Sources: IMF, *International Financial Statistics* and RFM backcast.

3

Current Account Forecasts

The relatively close adherence of the backcasts in figures 13 and 14 provides some basis for confidence that the RFM can provide useful forecasts. An important caveat is that the elements of the current account that are simply projected by linear trend are likely to yield larger errors the further out the prediction. As noted above, potentially (but not in practice through 1997) this is especially true from the standpoint of the model's straight-line projection of trends in factor services.

Before turning to the forecasts, it is useful to consider the principal elements that should be expected to drive the results. In the RFM, real exchange rates and levels of economic activity determine the path of the current account. It is appropriate, then, to begin with the impact of the change in the value of the dollar.[1]

Has the Dollar Collapsed?

The broad public impression has been that the dollar has plunged in recent years and especially in early 1995. It is thus understandable that even sophisticated observers might conclude that a major reduction is in store for the US external current account deficit.

However, a striking feature of the exchange rate series (figures 3 and 4, and tables 3 and 4) is that the real rate for the United States has been

1. The analysis of this chapter was prepared before the August 1995 rally in the dollar, which was heavily abetted by central bank intervention. For a discussion of the possible impact of the dollar's partial recovery, see chapter 4.

relatively flat for the past several years, in contrast to the dramatic decline of the REER from 1985 to 1987.[2] As noted above, the absence of a decline after about 1988 is even more complete for the real rate against developing countries (compiled from the Dallas Federal Reserve data). In contrast, there has indeed been a sharp increase for the real value of the yen, although this rise has been more dramatic when compared against the early 1990 temporary low than against the earlier post–Plaza Agreement high point of 1988.

For the dollar, the relatively flat profile in 1990–94 contradicts the popular notion that the dollar collapsed in this period. Instead, the REER against industrial country currencies remained close to an index of 97–98 for 1990–94 (table 3). Even in 1995 the value for the first quarter (set equal to the February level) was little changed. Only by the second quarter (estimated here with 11 April 1995 values) does the dollar decline substantially, from an index of 97.5 for 1994 as a whole to 90.6 for the second quarter of 1995. The latter value applies an exchange rate of 84.3 yen per dollar and 1.41 deutsche marks per dollar.

This broad constancy of the real trade-weighted dollar in recent years, until the second quarter of 1995, contrasts sharply with the currency's dramatic recent drop against the yen and the deutsche mark. From 1990 to April 1995, the dollar fell by 41.8 percent against the yen and by 13 percent against the mark in nominal terms. As inflation was about the same in the three countries, the real declines were comparable. It is the large decline of the dollar especially against the yen that is dominant in public discourse about the currency. Yet on a trade-weighted basis, the dollar barely moved over most of this period.

The reason is that other major trading partners have experienced depreciations against the dollar. Canada is by far the largest partner of the United States, and the US dollar appreciated against the Canadian dollar by 18 percent from 1990 to April 1995 even though Canadian inflation did not exceed that of the United States. There were major devaluations of the pound sterling, Italian lira, Spanish peseta, and Portuguese escudo associated with the problems of Europe's Exchange Rate Mechanism (ERM) in 1992–93. Thus, the pound sterling depreciated against the dollar by 15 percent from 1991 to 1993.

Even in the seeming rout of the dollar in March and April 1995, when the dollar fell against the yen by 17.5 percent and against the deutsche mark by 13 percent from the 1994 averages (and by 10 percent against the French franc), the new wide bands of ± 15 percent in the ERM meant

2. Note that the quarterly series shown in figure 3 is based on 1985 = 100. The annual series shown in table 3 is the 1985 series rechained to 1990 = 100. The IMF's revised series with a base of 1990 is somewhat different and yields a slightly lower relative level in 1985. The difference would appear to reflect changes in weights from the 1985 to the 1990 index in the IMF's calculations.

that weaker European currencies did not rise in lock step against the dollar. Thus, by 11 April, the decline of the dollar from 1994 averages was only 4 percent against the pound sterling, and the dollar actually rose by 7 percent against the lira.

The overall effect was that, despite the public impression of a collapsing US dollar by early 1995, the US currency had not moved much on a trade-weighted basis even against industrial country currencies. Only by the second quarter of 1995 was there substantial movement in the REER against these currencies, to a level about 7 percent below the 1994 level.

With respect to LDC currencies, the dollar rose sharply against the Mexican peso in real terms in early 1995. However, as shown in figure 3, the real exchange rate of the dollar against LDC currencies overall stood unchanged by the second quarter of 1995 from its 1994 year-average level because the dollar's real decline against Pacific NIC and South American currencies offset the dollar's rise against the Mexican peso. During the first half of the 1990s, the share of industrial countries in US nonoil trade has been about 60 percent, and the share of LDCs, 40 percent. Using these weights, *by the second quarter of 1995 the overall real value of the dollar was only 4.2 percent below the average level for 1994 as a whole.* On this trade-weighted basis, the dollar had not collapsed.

Qualitative Outlook

Given the moderate real decline of the dollar, it might be expected that the US current account deficit would not necessarily be headed for correction, despite recent exchange rate trends. Two additional considerations strengthen this possibility. The first is the "gap factor." The second is the past tendency for US imports to rise more rapidly than US exports even with an unchanged real exchange rate against industrial country currencies (subject to the new finding in this study that this adverse trend may have been attributable to secular real appreciation against LDC currencies).

It is well known that the gap between exports and imports of a country starting from trade deficit (or surplus) is likely to cause that deficit (surplus) to balloon over time if there is no force to deflect this trajectory (Marris 1985). The reason is essentially that an equiproportionate growth of both imports and exports will cause an identical proportionate increase in the absolute gap between them, so that the absolute trade gap widens even with "normal" growth on both sides. As for the trends in imports and exports, any Houthakker-Magee asymmetry in income elasticities will mean erosion from this standpoint as well.

If we combine these considerations with the information that on a trade-weighted basis the US currency did not change much during 1990–94, and if we further take into account the boom in the US economy in

1993–94, contrasted with the bust in the Japanese economy and the only mediocre recovery in Europe by 1994, we should not expect a major reduction in the US current account deficit. Indeed, these trends are all consistent with what has occurred in the 1990s, with the US current account deficit widening from $68 billion in 1992 to $156 billion in 1994. The principal question today is whether the more significant decline in the dollar by the second quarter of 1995, perhaps in combination with more robust recovery abroad, will be sufficient to halt and even reverse the widening of the deficit.

The short-run answer is, one should expect the US current account deficit to get larger in 1995, not smaller. The first reason is that in 1993 the real dollar appreciated by 4.5 percent against industrial country currencies, moving from an index (REER) of 94.3 in 1992 to 98.5 (table 3). The standard two-year lag would suggest that this phenomenon would cause a widening of the deficit in 1995, other things being equal. A second reason is that in 1995 there will be a large impact of the Mexican peso crisis on the US trade balance. A third reason is that the factor services assessment is deteriorating at about $8 billion per year (table 2).

Over the medium term, however, there could be a reduction in the estimated deficit from the 1995 level if the lagged impact of the 1995 dollar depreciation, and the effect of possible recovery in Japan, outweigh any secular trend tendencies caused by the gap factor, income elasticity asymmetries, and cumulative factor services deterioration. These trends are examined in detail in the "impact" analysis below.

Forecast Assumptions

To go beyond these qualitative considerations to a 1995–97 forecast using the RFM developed here, it is necessary to project three variables: domestic and foreign GDP, and the real exchange rate. If we assume that the April exchange rates hold,[3] then the sequence of lagged quarterly real exchange rates is already known, and thus so is the impact of the real exchange rate variable through 1997. As for the nominal exchange rate and the ratio of foreign to domestic prices, freezing the real exchange rate and assuming equal inflation domestically and in the other industrial countries permits setting these variables unchanged at their second quarter 1995 levels.[4]

The IMF's (1994a) forecasts for 1995 GDP are applied to determine the path of relative GDP. These rates are 2.5 percent for the United States,

3. By mid-August 1995 the yen was back to 97 to the dollar and the deutsche mark to 1.48 to the dollar. The central forecasts here thus assume that this reversal was a temporary blip.

4. With the assumption of unchanged domestic prices, the real and nominal effective exchange rates (REER and NEER) change by the same proportion from first quarter 1995 to second quarter 1995 before their steady state.

3.8 percent for Canada, and 2.8 percent for Europe. For Japan, the forecast here is downgraded to 2 percent for 1995, in view of the weak recovery and the added pressure from yen appreciation. For 1996 and 1997, growth is set at 2.5 percent in the United States, Canada, and Europe. The rate for Japan is assumed to rebound to 4.5 percent in 1996 and 4 percent in 1997. For developing countries, the growth rate (weighted by US exports) is set at 3.3 percent for 1995 and rebounds to 4.9 percent in 1996–97 with Mexican recovery.

It should be stressed that the growth assumptions for Japan are on the generous side. Thus the Blue Chip (1995) consensus forecast of approximately 50 private forecasting firms places growth for Japan at 1.1 percent in 1995 and 2.4 percent in 1996. Slower growth than presumed here would mean a larger Japanese current account surplus and less external adjustment by 1997. However, slow growth would also mean that Japan's output remained well below potential. To some extent, policy evaluations of external-sector outcomes might appropriately be judged on a "cyclically adjusted" basis, much as the usual diagnosis of fiscal stance involves a standardized-employment estimate rather than simply the observed level. Even so, leaning too far in the direction of excusing a large Japanese current account surplus on grounds of domestic recession would in turn raise the question of whether it was appropriate for Japan to "export unemployment," especially if several other major countries faced slack demand.

The Mexico Factor

The Mexican peso crisis of December 1994 is likely to have a major impact on the US current account balance in 1995, beyond the effects likely to be captured in the RFM. The government seeks to cut Mexico's external current account deficit from nearly $30 billion in 1994 to nearly zero in 1995. Extremely high interest rates adopted in part to attract foreign capital mean increased incidence of bankruptcies, pressure on the banking system, and recessionary pressure. Real wages are likely to decline significantly, as the minimum wage increase for 1995 is to lag far behind expected inflation. Real growth for 1995 could be as low as −4 percent.

The impact on the US external balance for 1995 seems likely to be on the order of −$20 billion. Of Mexico's total trade turnover, 73.5 percent is conducted with the United States (IMF 1995b). A reduction of $30 billion in Mexico's current account deficit would thus be expected to reduce the US external balance by $22 billion if marginal trade shares are the same as average.

The RFM captures the Mexico effect primarily through the movement in the Dallas Fed real exchange rate for LDCs. For the second quarter of 1995 (April) against the 1994 average, the real exchange rate for the dollar against the peso rose by 48 percent. Given Mexico's weight in the LDC real exchange rate r^*, there was a corresponding partial increase of 6.7 percent in this rate.[5] Applying this increase to the export base for goods and services, the initial import/export ratio, and the coefficient on the LDC real exchange rate r^* in both the DC and LDC trade equations (π_6 in table 1), the result is a surprisingly large model estimate of the Mexico impact (after all lags are exhausted) equaling a $47 billion reduction in the US external account.[6] This impact shows the model's sensitivity to the LDC exchange rate.[7]

Because of the RFM's two-year lag structure, the Mexico impact tends to be understated in 1995 (one-sixth of the full eventual impact, or −$7 billion). However, the ultimate effect would seem overstated, even allowing for the fact that the comparison is against a baseline that otherwise would have shown a widening US surplus with Mexico at unchanged exchange rates. On this basis, the forecast below includes a variant adjusted for the Mexico impact, in which the US current account deficit is increased by $13 billion in 1995 above the level otherwise calculated (i.e, the informal estimate of a $20 billion shock, less the $7 billion captured by the trade equations); left unchanged in 1996; and decreased by $10 billion from the level otherwise calculated in 1997.[8]

A Consensus Model

From the large literature on US trade elasticities, it is possible to synthesize a "consensus model" constructed along the same lines as that proposed here but forcing parameters to values consistent with those typically found in the literature. This approach could be especially helpful in checking the influence of the pass-through coefficients, which as suggested above and in the appendix are not robustly estimated here. It can also provide a check on the projections of the RFM by introducing some element of US income elasticity asymmetry, a standard finding in the literature that is not found to hold in the estimates here.

Hooper and Marquez (1995) have reviewed the trade model literature. Among 37 such studies, the median price elasticity for US exports is 1.31

---

5. Overall there was no change in r^* from the 1994 average to the second quarter of 1995. The decline of the dollar against the Pacific NIC and Other Latin America currencies offset the move against the Mexican peso.

6. For a discussion of impact calculations more generally, see the discussion below and the estimates in table 5.

7. The $47 billion steady-state impact is estimated as $26 billion in US-LDC trade and $21 billion in US-DC trade. However, Mexico is a minor competitor in industrial country markets, so the latter is no doubt overstated.

8. Without this adjustment, the partial impact of Mexico reaches −$34 billion in 1996 and −$47 billion in 1997.

and for US imports, 1.35. They note that most studies show US import-price pass-through at 50 to 70 percent, and export-price pass-through at 80 to 100 percent. In new estimates of their own, the two authors place the import-price pass-through at 55 percent and export pass-through at 84 percent. They also obtain new estimates of the income elasticity of imports at 2.5 and of exports at 1.0. However, estimates by Lawrence (1990) suggest a central value for the import income elasticity of 2.0.

To construct a consensus model with the data set used in this study, it is first necessary to aggregate the model variables into overall measures, because the standard parameters do not distinguish between industrial country and LDC trade. For the dependent variable (nonoil imports of goods and nonfactor services relative to exports of goods and nonfactor services), the aggregate ratio is simply the original data before disaggregation (described above). For the aggregate real exchange rate, a weighted average of the REER for the industrial countries (R^*) and the Dallas Fed rate for the developing countries (r^*) is obtained, using 1987 total US trade turnover with the two areas for weighting. For the aggregate foreign income variable, the DC and LDC income variables are weighted by 1987 US exports to each respective area.

The weighted average nominal exchange rate (R) is more complicated, because although the nominal rate enters into the DC equation, it is not used in the LDC equation. Implicitly the LDC model assumes there is no difference between domestic and trade prices, because there is complete pass-through. As a result, the implicit nominal exchange rate is always equal to the real exchange rate. Accordingly, the weighted average nominal rate used for the consensus model is composed of the DC nominal rate (R) weighted by 1987 US trade turnover with DCs, plus the LDC *real* exchange rate (r^*)—which by assumption equals the hypothetical nominal rate for LDCs—weighted by US trade turnover with LDCs.

Similarly, since the ratio of foreign price to domestic price (P_f/P_d) is calculated by dividing the real exchange rate into the nominal exchange rate, the weighted average DC-LDC price ratio is the DC ratio weighted by US trade turnover with DCs, plus a simple constant index of 100 for LDCs weighted by turnover with LDCs. The latter measure of the price ratio derives from the fact that the ratio of the implicit LDC nominal exchange rate to the real exchange rate is always unity.

With these aggregate variables in hand, it is then possible to estimate equation 16 with constrained values assigned to the "consensus" parameters. These are: $\phi = 1.35$, $\beta = -1.31$, $\rho = -0.55$, $\epsilon = -0.16$, $\theta = 2.0$, and $\gamma = -1.0$. Incorporating these parameters into their corresponding regression model coefficients (π_1 through π_5), and shifting all of these "knowns" to the left-hand side, the resulting regression simply determines the optimal constant and quarterly dummies for the best fit with the data. As in the other cases, the estimate uses Cochrane-Orcutt first-order autoregression.

Figure 15 United States: RFM consensus model backcast of trade ratio[a]

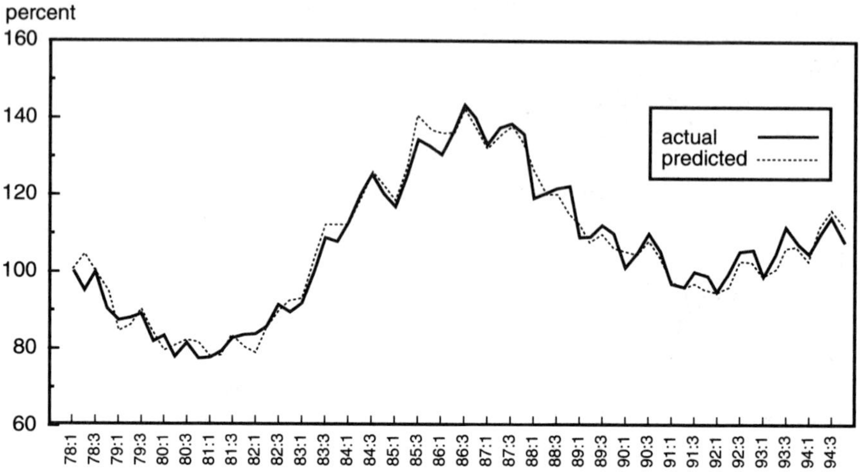

a. Ratio of nonoil imports of goods and nonfactor services to exports of goods and nonfactor services.

Figure 15 shows the backcast for the import/export ratio using this "consensus" model. The figure suggests that this model does relatively well in explaining the past behavior of the US trade ratio. It should therefore serve as a helpful check on the RFM for forecasting purposes.

EAG Model

Another basis for confirming the RFM projections is to project the larger EAG model (Cline 1989). The forecasts reported below include this projection under the assumptions just outlined.

Projections

With recalibration to the actual outcome for 1994, the forecast of the main version of the RFM under the above assumptions calls for the US current account to deteriorate to a deficit of $172 billion in 1995 (table 5, RFM1).[9] There is a modest improvement by 1996–97 in response to the decline of

9. To adjust for divergence of the trendline factor services estimate in 1994 from the actual outcome, a constant of $4 billion is subtracted in the projections of table 5. There is also a scalar multiple of 1.0116 applied to the import/export ratio to achieve model adherence to the actual 1994 outcome (in comparison with model projection for 1994 using fourth quarter 1993 as the last observation for the autoregressive dependent variable).

Table 5 Alternative current account projections, 1994–97
(billions of dollars)

	1994	1995	1996	1997
United States				
RFM1	−157	−172	−160	−162
RFM2	−157	−185	−160	−152
RFM-CNS	−157	−175	−152	−157
EAG	−165	−202	−183	−183
IMF	•	−178	−179	•
Actual	−156	•	•	•
Japan				
RFM	123	111	95	87
EAG	106	127	90	87
IMF	•	129	128	•
Actual	129	•	•	•

RFM1 = basic RFM forecast
RFM2 = adjustment for Mexico
RFM-CNS = consensus model
EAG = External Adjustment with Growth model (Cline 1989)
IMF = International Monetary Fund (1995c)

the dollar in the second quarter of 1995 and higher foreign growth, and the deficit falls to $162 billion by 1997. It should be reiterated that these baseline forecasts assume real exchange rates of second-quarter 1995, and thus imply that the August 1995 dollar rally will prove transitory.

If the RFM is adjusted to take into account a more realistic profile of the impact of the Mexican peso crisis (variant RFM2), the result is to boost the US current account deficit for 1995 to $185 billion but to reduce the 1997 estimated deficit to $152 billion (for the reasons discussed above). However, it is ambiguous whether the Mexico-adjusted projection is superior because in a probabilistic sense there could be other random influences in trade with other countries working in directions that offset the unique Mexico effects.

For its part, the consensus version of the RFM (RFM-CNS) yields a current account deficit that is slightly larger than the basic RFM1 estimate for 1995 but slightly smaller in 1996–97. As discussed below in the impact analysis of the models, the consensus model has a more sensitive response to the real exchange rate. Consequently, its 1995 reaction to the 1993 dollar appreciation is greater and so is its 1997 reaction to the 1995 depreciation. Partly offsetting this difference by 1997 is the adverse influence of income elasticity asymmetry in RFM-CNS, absent in RFM1.

The RFM1, RFM2, and RFM-CNS projections represent two pieces of bad news and one of good news. The first bad news is that the current account deficit is likely to widen to the range of $180 billion in 1995, or 2.5 percent of GDP. A record deficit is thus in store for 1995 in absolute nominal-dollar terms. Relative to GDP, the deficit would remain considerably below the peak of 3.6 percent reached in 1987. Still, the deficit would be far above a more desirable target of perhaps 1 percent of GDP, as suggested by Williamson (1985) and further developed below in an alternative formulation.

The second piece of bad news is that despite the seemingly major adjustment of the dollar by mid-1995, there is only meager external adjustment in the pipeline even after 1995. The RFM1, RFM2, and RFM-CNS range of $152 billion to $162 billion by 1997 would still represent 1.9 to 2.0 percent of GDP in that year, almost twice as large as the target level.

The good news amounts to cold comfort: the RFM projections are not quite as unfavorable as the other projections used for benchmark comparison in table 5. The EAG model shows the 1995 current account deficit rising to $202 billion, and little improvement thereafter (with the deficit still over $180 billion by 1997). Although not shown in the table, it is of some use to consider what might be called a "window" forecast for 1995 (based on the cardinal rule among weather forecasters to look out the window before issuing their short-term predictions). Based on simple extrapolation of trends in the first six months of 1995, the current account deficit for the year would also reach $202 billion—at the EAG's upper end of the range in table 5.[10]

The International Monetary Fund (1995) forecasts a deficit of $178 billion for 1995, squarely in the middle of the RFM field. But the IMF figure for 1996 remains at $179 billion, whereas the RFM variants drop to $160 billion or slightly less. (The organization does not forecast beyond the next year.) In view of the IMF projections, it is curious that the managing director of the IMF, Michel Camdessus, has argued that the dollar fell too far in early 1995 and that US authorities should have raised interest rates to push the currency up again (*Wall Street Journal*, 19 April 1995). As discussed below, if the dollar had not declined in the first half of 1995, much larger deficits would have arisen by 1997.

The main reason for the more favorable baseline in the RFM1 and RFM2 projections than in the EAG model is that the model estimated in table

10. In January through June 1995, US exports of goods and nonfactor services rose by 13.2 percent above their level in the same period of 1994 (US Department of Commerce 1995e). Nonoil imports rose by 14.8 percent, and oil imports by 18.9 percent. Applied to the 1994 base (Commerce Department definitions), these rates would mean an increase in the deficit on goods and nonfactor services from $106.2 billion to $135.2 billion in 1995. The corresponding balance-of-payments (and RFM) definition would thus show an increase in the goods and nonfactor services deficit from $123 billion to $152 billion. Comparison of data for the first quarter of 1995 against the first quarter of 1994 shows an increase of 46.8 percent in factor services income, 37.5 percent in factor services payments, and 5.6 percent in net transfers (US Department of Commerce 1995c). At these rates of change, the full-year balances would reach −$14 billion for net factor services, and −$36 billion for transfers. The overall current account deficit would reach $202 billion.

1 has almost no Houthakker-Magee asymmetry in income elasticities. In contrast, there is a modest difference between the import and export income elasticities in the EAG model, and this differential is unity in the consensus (RFM-CNS) model. In comparison with RFM-CNS, the EAG model is more pessimistic by 1997 not so much because of different parameters (the income elasticity asymmetry is more comparable) but because EAG has regional detail and more fully captures the consequences of the Mexico devaluation.

Whereas the RFM forecast for the United States shows further widening of the external imbalance (albeit only in 1995), the projection for Japan shows an important reduction in the imbalance. As shown in table 5, Japan's current account surplus drops from a model estimate of $123 billion in 1994 (actual figure, $129 billion) to $111 billion in 1995 and only $87 billion by 1997. The driving force in this outcome is the remarkable trade-weighted real appreciation of the yen. With an index of 100 for 1990, the real yen rose by about 10 percent by 1992, and then surged to 129 in 1993, 138 in 1994, and 156 by April 1995 (figure 4 and table 4). Given the predominant role of the real exchange rate in the RFM, this path understandably generates a significant adjustment after the two-year lag. The projection for Japan does assume that the strong yen does not derail recovery to growth lower than 2 percent in 1995, and the forecast is also vulnerable to the likelihood that Japan's growth could be well below the 4 to 4½ percent range assumed here for 1996–97.

The RFM forecast for Japan is somewhat more favorable than most projections, in terms of downward adjustment of the excessive surplus. The IMF (1995c) calls for Japan's current account surplus to remain unchanged at $129.5 billion in 1995 and $127.7 billion in 1996.

Impact Parameters

How would alternative changes in the exchange rate and growth affect the RFM predictions? To identify the impact of changes in these variables, first define z as the ratio of the value of nonoil imports of goods and nonfactor services to exports of goods and nonfactor services. From equation 16, as augmented by the cross-price term and suppressing the lag operator to obtain steady-state impact, we have:

$$\frac{\partial \ln z}{\partial \ln R^*} = \pi_1 + \pi_2 \frac{\partial \ln R}{\partial \ln R^*} + \pi_5 \frac{\partial \ln R}{\partial \ln R^*} + \pi_6 \frac{\partial \ln r^*}{\partial \ln R^*} + \frac{\partial \ln[P_f / P_d]}{\partial \ln R^*} \quad (21)$$

If we are prepared to assume that domestic producers do not change their home prices in response to exchange rate changes, so that P_f / P_d is invariant with respect to the real (and nominal) exchange rate, then the final term in equation 21 is zero. From the definition of the real exchange rate in equation 1, the second and third right-hand-side derivatives are unity: the nominal exchange rate varies proportionately with the real exchange rate (again assuming no induced changes in domestic prices).

To examine the impact of a generalized change in the dollar against all industrial and developing-country currencies, it may further be assumed that the fourth right-hand-side derivative is unity (because of identical proportionate change in r^* and R^*). The result is that the derivative of the logarithm of the import/export ratio (z) with respect to the logarithm of the real exchange rate equals the sum of the four regression parameters: $\pi_1 + \pi_2 + \pi_5 + \pi_6$. As the derivative of the logarithm is equal to the proportionate change, this means that the elasticity of the import/export ratio with respect to the real exchange rate equals the sum of these four parameters.[11]

Translating the regression parameters into their analytical equivalents, we have:

$$\eta_{zR^*} = [\phi - \beta] - [\phi(1+\rho) + \beta\epsilon] + [\rho - \epsilon] + [\psi - \Omega] \qquad (22)$$

where η_{zR^*} is the elasticity of the import/export ratio with respect to the real exchange rate. The first term on the right-hand side is straightforward: higher trade price elasticities mean a higher elasticity for the import/export ratio with respect to the real exchange rate. The final term means just the same thing, but with respect to the influence of cross-price effects relative to developing country suppliers in the industrial country market.

The second and third terms are less transparent and refer to the influence of the pass-through from exchange rate changes to trade prices. When pass-through is complete, the second term becomes zero and the third term becomes minus unity. This negative unity captures the traditional Marshall-Lerner effect of what must be subtracted from volume change to obtain value change when the exchange rate changes. Hence the condition that the sum of trade price elasticities must exceed unity if trade values are to respond in the desired direction to exchange rate change.

When pass-through is less than complete, the effects are more complicated and will depend on the sizes of the import and export price elasticities. If we designate the sum of the second and third terms as *PTL* for pass-through leakage, then the impact of these two terms has the following characteristics.[12] First, when both the import and export price elasticities

---

11. For US trade with LDCs, following the parallel interpretation of equation 19 as augmented by the cross-price term, we have the result that the derivative of z with respect to r^* equals $\lambda_1 + \lambda_4$, where λ_4 is the parameter on R^*_L. In terms of table 1, for US-LDC trade this elasticity is $\pi_1 + \pi_6$.

12. Based on numerical investigation with a range of ϕ and $|\beta|$ each from 0.6 to 1.5, and at 0.1 intervals for ρ and ϵ from 0 to -1.

are unitary, *PTL* is always -1. Second, when the import price elasticity is less than unity, lower pass-through ratios reduce *PTL* in absolute size. With quantity response inelastic, induced price offsets have less impact in dampening the trade impact that would otherwise occur. Third, conversely, when the import price elasticity is greater than unity, lower pass-through increases the *PTL*. Lower pass-through means less chance for the exchange rate change to affect prices, and quantities are responsive to price changes. Fourth, when the import-price elasticity is unity, for a given export pass-through ratio the *PTL* is identical whatever the import pass-through. Fifth, when the export-price elasticity is unity, for a given import pass-through the *PTL* is identical whatever the export pass-through. Fifth, if $\phi + |\beta| = k$, $PTL \leq k - 1$. This relationship means that the Marshall-Lerner requirement will always be met by a wider margin when there is incomplete pass-through than when there is complete pass-through.

Table 6 reports the impact parameters from the RFM estimates reported in table 1. For the exchange rate, a real depreciation of the dollar by 1 percent against DC and LDC currencies reduces the US external deficit by $12.6 billion after lags are completed. This estimate is broadly comparable to the $10 billion per percent impact in the EAG model (Cline 1989, 209).[13]

A 1 percentage point increase in domestic growth over one year reduces the US current account balance by $10 billion in the RFM. In comparison, the figure from the EAG model is $14.8 billion. The difference reflects a lower income elasticity for imports in the RFM (about 1.2, weighted) than in the EAG model (2.2).[14] Thus, the absence of Houthakker-Magee asymmetry in the RFM, which is more optimistic for long-term trends, also means that there is less scope for "adjustment" of external deficits through domestic recession.

A generalized increase in foreign growth by 1 percentage point over one year improves the US external balance by $9.2 billion. This impact is smaller than the $11.5 billion estimate in the EAG model, which has a higher income elasticity for US exports.[15]

The corresponding impact parameters for Japan are $2.1 billion per percent on the real exchange rate, $2.7 billion per percentage-point-year on domestic growth, and $3.0 billion per percentage-point-year on foreign growth. These estimates are smaller than in the EAG model ($3.7 billion per percent on the real exchange rate and $5 billion per percentage-point-

13. The EAG parameters are specified in impacts by 1992 from variable changes in 1989. The RFM parameters are for 1997 changes from variable changes in 1995, and so refer to a higher nominal base.

14. The EAG projections take the average of country-specific elasticities (2.44 for US income elasticity on imports) and global averages (1.97).

15. Direct estimate, 1.69; averaged with global average, 1.83 (Cline 1989, 172).

Table 6 Impact parameters: RFM, CNS, and EAG models

		United States			Japan	
Symbol	Concept	RFM	CNS	EAG	RFM	EAG
$\hat{X}_o$	Exports base (1994, G&S, $bn)	•	687	•	436	•
	DC	398	•	•	•	•
	LDC	289	•	•	•	•
z_o	Nonoil trade ratio base	•	1.105	•	0.685	•
	DC	1.140	•	•	•	•
	LDC	1.031	•	•	•	•
$\pi_1 + \pi_2 + \pi_5 + \pi_6$	Real exchange rate elasticity	•	1.46	•	0.694	•
	DC	1.386	•	•	•	•
	LDC	2.132	•	•	•	•
$\Delta B_{R^*_1}$	Impact of 1% change in real exchange rate ($bn) $= -\hat{X}_o z_o[\pi_1 + \pi_2 + \pi_5 + \pi_6][.01]$	−12.6	−11.1	−10.9	−2.1	−3.7
ΔB_{gd}	Impact of increase in domestic growth rate by 1% for 1 year $= -\hat{X}_o z_o \pi_3[.01]$ ($bn)	−9.9	−15.2	−16.8	−2.7	−5.1
ΔB_{gf}	Impact of increase in foreign growth rate by 1% for 1 year $-\hat{X}_o z_o \pi_4[.01]$ ($bn)	9.2	7.6	13.1	3.0	•

ΔB_{gt}	Secular growth drift [a] $= \Delta B_{gd} g_d + \Delta B_{gf(ldc)} g_{ldc} + \Delta B_{gf(dc)} g_{dc}$ (\$bn)	6.7	−10.0	−4.9	−5.0	•
ΔB_{GAP}	Gap factor annual effect $= r\hat{X}_o[1 - z_o]$ (\$bn)	−4.9	−4.9	−4.9	9.6	•
ΔB_{FS}	Secular factor services drift (table 2) \$bn	−7.5	−7.5	−7.5	2.9	•
ΔB_{SD}	Overall secular drift (\$bn) $= \Delta B_{gt} + \Delta B_{GAP} + \Delta B_{FS}$	−5.7	−22.4	−17.3	7.5	•

a. For US: $g_d = 2.5\%$, $g_{dc} = 2.7\%$, and $g_{ldc} = 4.9\%$.
For Japan: $g_d = 4\%$, $g_f = 2.5\%$

RFM = Reduced Form Model
CNS = Consensus Model
EAG = External Adjustment with Growth Model

year on domestic growth).[16] For the exchange rate, the discrepancy may reflect the fact that the RFM incorporates incomplete pass-through whereas the EAG model assumes complete pass-through. For both effects, there is the additional difference that the EAG model cumulates factor service feedback effects from changes in cumulative current account deficits, whereas the RFM does not.

The last four entries in table 6 examine the secular drift in the external accounts. The first element in this drift stems from the combined influences of income elasticity asymmetry and differences between domestic and foreign growth. It turns out that with the RFM results of minimal elasticity asymmetry for the United States, the fact that foreign growth (including that of LDCs) somewhat exceeds US growth means that there is actually a favorable US secular drift from the standpoint of growth impact. For Japan, this impact is, ironically, negative because Japan is assumed to grow more rapidly by 1996–97 than its industrial country counterparts.[17]

The gap factor works in the opposite direction. Proportionate growth for both imports and exports causes the US external balance to worsen by about $5 billion each year, and the Japanese balance to increase by almost $10 billion annually. Similarly, the annual change in the factor services balance calculated from the linear trends in table 2 means a further yearly reduction of the US external balance by $7.5 billion and an increase in the Japanese balance by about $3 billion.

Overall, the combined effects yield what might be called the "GAF" secular trend: for the gap factor (G), elasticity asymmetry (A), and factor services (F) trend on cumulating net foreign assets or liabilities. In the RFM, there is a negative secular GAF drift of almost $6 billion annually in the US accounts and a positive secular GAF drift of $7.5 billion in the Japanese external account. In view of the real exchange rate impact parameters, these secular trends suggest that there could be a need for the US dollar to depreciate in real terms by about 0.5 percent annually ($6 billion/$12.6 billion per percent) just to hold the external deficit constant, and a corresponding need for the Japanese yen to appreciate in real terms by as much as 3.5 percent annually ($7.5 billion/$2.08 billion per percent) to keep the Japanese surplus from rising. The alternative estimates using the EAG parameters would be a 0.6 percent slide of the real dollar and a 2 percent upward glide for the real yen.

There is the further question of whether a secular real appreciation of the dollar against LDC currencies should be added onto the baseline (which, in the forecasts, assumes instead that real exchange rates remain

16. Calculated from Cline (1989, 211), based on percentage of exports of goods and nonfactor services, as applied to the 1994 trade base.

17. The foreign growth rate in the Japan estimates is only for the OECD. If LDCs had been included, the export income elasticity would have tended to be lower because the foreign income growth rate would have been higher.

constant). A parallel question is how much such a trend would contribute to annual slide in the US external accounts. From a base in 1978–80 to a terminal period of 1992–94, the real US exchange rate against LDCs rose by 23 percent, for an average annual increase of 1.5 percent.

Calculation of a separate impact parameter for the LDC exchange rate indicates a $7.1 billion effect of a 1 percent change.[18] If there were to be a persistent 1.5 percent real appreciation of the dollar against LDC currencies in the future, there would be an additional adverse slide of the US current account balance amounting to about $10 billion annually from this source. The corresponding constant-deficit slide of the weighted real dollar would then amount to [$16 billion/$12.6 billion] ≈ 1.25 percent per year. With the dollar rising at 1.5 percent against LDC currencies, and with a weight of about 0.4 on these currencies, it would then require a secular decline of the dollar of about 3 percent per year against DC currencies to attain the required weighted-average decline of 1.25 percent per year.

It would seem inappropriate to assume a continued secular rise of the dollar against LDC exchange rates, and indeed the real rate against these currencies has been relatively flat since 1988 (figure 3). However, these calculations highlight the importance of taking the real exchange rate against LDC trading partners into account, and they suggest that there could be a more unfavorable structural tendency of the US current account than the RFM's $6 billion annual slide estimated table 6 if the dollar did revert to a long-term rise against these currencies.

For comparison, table 6 also reports impact parameters for the EAG and consensus models. The real exchange rate impact is comparable in these two models to that in the RFM. All three show that a 1 percent change in the real exchange rate causes a change of $11 billion to $12.5 billion in the US external account. The models show more divergence on the growth parameters, however, because of the varying degrees of presence of the Houthakker-Magee elasticity asymmetry. The consensus model shows a $15 billion change with each percentage-point-year change in US domestic growth, and the EAG model, almost $17 billion.[19] In the consensus model, additional foreign growth of 1 percentage point improves the balance by $7.6 billion, but the EAG improvement is considerably larger ($13.1 billion).

Applying expected growth rates domestically and abroad, the resulting secular growth drift from income elasticity asymmetry is about −$5 billion annually in EAG and −$10 billion in the consensus model, a sharp contrast to the +$6.7 billion drift in the RFM. Adding secular drift from

---

18. Or: [$398 billion × 1.14 × 0.709 × .01] + [$289 billion × 1.03 × 1.316 × .01]; see table 6.

19. The parameter here is derived from the EAG impact estimated as a fraction of exports of goods and nonfactor services (Cline 1989, 211), as applied to the 1994 export base.

the gap factor and factor-services erosion places overall GAF drift at −$17.3 billion annually in EAG and −$22.4 billion in the consensus model.

The EAG and consensus models are thus more pessimistic than the RFM. It is accordingly no surprise that the EAG model gives a more unfavorable projection for 1997 than the RFM (table 5). It is a surprise that the consensus model shows a slightly more favorable current account by 1997 than the RFM despite a much larger adverse drift. The explanation appears to be that the bulk of the real depreciation of the dollar in 1995 is against the industrial country currencies, and by applying an average depreciation to the aggregate exchange rate elasticity, RFM-CNS gives a larger exchange rate response than does RFM1, which takes specific account of the DC versus LDC exchange rate.[20]

The large adverse secular drifts in the US accounts in the consensus model and, to a lesser degree, the EAG model, do suggest that, by 1998 and after, there might be significant worsening of the external account in the absence of changes from the baseline. The two alternative models suggest that the RFM may err on the optimistic side over the medium term, perhaps implying that the possibility of adverse secular drift in the LDC real exchange rate (discussed above) is a significant downside risk.

For Japan, table 6 shows substantially higher exchange rate and growth impact parameters in the EAG model than in RFM. A 1 percent change in the exchange rate induces $3.7 billion in external adjustment and 1 percentage-point-year on domestic growth, a $5 billion change. The EAG model also shows a larger reduction in the external surplus from 1995 to 1997 than does RFM, tending to reinforce the RFM conclusion of significant Japanese adjustment by 1997.

Finally, in the spirit of impact analysis, it is instructive to simulate the RFM under the assumption that the dollar had stayed unchanged at its 1994 average real level rather than declining against industrial country currencies in the first half of 1995. When this is done, the result is a projected current account deficit of $210 billion by 1997. Thus, in the absence of the decline of the dollar in the first half of 1995, the external deficit would have been about $50 billion higher by 1997 than in the baseline scenario. This difference is consistent with the parameter of $12.6 billion per percentage point, combined with the fact that in the baseline there was zero change of the real exchange rate against LDCs in the second quarter of 1995 and after from the 1994 average, but a 7.1 percent real decline for the real exchange rate against industrial countries. With

20. In RFM, almost 60 percent of a uniform exchange rate impact is from LDC trade, whereas only 40 percent of trade is with LDCs. With the LDC real rate approximately constant and the dollar's decline focused on industrial country exchange rates, the result is that the aggregate RFM-CNS formulation gives more adjustment from the 1995 depreciation than does RFM1.

a nonoil trade turnover of 59.3 percent for DCs, the weighted-average decline of the dollar in 1995 from 1994 amounts to 4.2 percent, which yields approximately a $50 billion impact when multiplied by the exchange rate impact parameter.[21]

For Japan, if the real exchange rate had remained unchanged at its 1994 level, the RFM predicts that by 1997 the current account surplus would have stood at $109 billion rather than falling to $87 billion. Given the 13 percent real appreciation over the 1994 average, the implicit impact parameter is $1.7 billion per percentage point on the real exchange rate ([$109 billion–$87 billion]/ 13 percent), modestly lower than in the direct calculation of table 6.[22]

21. The simple product is somewhat larger, but there is a proportionately somewhat stronger exchange rate impact for the LDC real exchange rate, so the impact parameter approach yields a larger change than does comparison of the alternative simulations.

22. For such a large percentage change in the real exchange rate, the average (''arc'') elasticity is noticeably smaller than the marginal (''point'') elasticity.

4

Conclusion

Implications of the Analysis

The Reduced Form Model (RFM) developed here should provide a useful vehicle for frequent, timely current account forecasts for the United States and Japan. The model is simpler and more transparent, and the data requirements much less demanding, than is the case for more typical current account models. The linear time trends for factor services and transfers can be easily updated. The core equation for the import/export ratio is also easy to update, as most of its variables are reported on a relatively timely basis by the International Monetary Fund in its *International Financial Statistics* (REER) and *World Economic Outlook* (relative GDP). The model does require the construction of a weighted average of LDC real exchange rates against the dollar using estimates prepared by the Dallas Federal Reserve. Despite its simplicity, the RFM provides a good explanation of the current accounts of the United States and Japan over the sample period 1980–94 (figures 13 and 14), and indeed does a better job than the EAG in tracking recent Japanese experience.

The RFM (adjusted for Mexico effects) and the multicountry EAG model indicate that in 1995 the US current account deficit is likely to deteriorate to between \$180 billion and \$200 billion, and the International Monetary Fund has placed the outcome at the lower end of this range (table 5). One important reason for the sharp deterioration in 1995 is that there was a real appreciation of the dollar from 1992 to 1993 by almost 5 percent on a trade-weighted basis relative to industrial countries. The trade outcome for 1995 will reflect the customary two-year lag from that exchange rate signal. A second key influence on the 1995 outcome will be the Mexico shock, responsible for perhaps a $20 billion deterioration in the accounts. A third influence is the deterioration in the capital services balance by about $8 billion annually as the United States goes deeper into international debt.

The RFM variants, including those with special adjustments for Mexico and using the "consensus" instead of directly estimated coefficients, then show the US current account deficit leveling off at about $160 billion by 1996–97.[1] The moderation of the deficit is even less in the EAG projections. The extent of the prospective improvement after 1995 will be disappointing to many observers in view of the perception that the dollar has declined sharply in 1995. Yet even the improvement by 1997 in the forecasts of table 5 assumes that the dollar stays at the April 1995 level, and thus that the August dollar rally will prove to be transitory.

The seeming contradiction of limited improvement with the stylized fact of already enormous dollar depreciation is largely explained by the reality that on a trade-weighted basis the dollar has not fallen much in recent years. Even after the sharp slide against the deutsche mark and yen in March and April 1995, by the second quarter of 1995 the real value of the dollar against industrial country currencies stood only about 7 percent below its 1994 level, and that level in turn had been equal to the 1990–93 average. The reason for the modest overall depreciation despite the sharp drop against key currencies (17.5 percent against the yen and 13 percent against the deutsche mark, from the 1994 average to mid-April 1995)[2] was that there had been a large appreciation against the Canadian dollar (and Canada is the most important trading partner of the United States) and that weaker European currencies had not appreciated nearly as much against the dollar as had the deutsche mark and yen. Against developing-country currencies, the dollar stood unchanged in the second

1. In an earlier version of this study, as reported in the *Wall Street Journal* (24 April 1995), the RFM projection for 1997 was a range of $171 billion to $192 billion. However, that formulation of the model lacked two major improvements. First, it did not explicitly incorporate the lagged nominal exchange rate as an explanatory variable. Second, it did not separate out US trade with industrial and developing countries, and worked only with the DC REER rather than incorporating the LDC real exchange rate as well. The driving force behind the less unfavorable result in the revised model is that incorporation of these two improvements removes the income elasticity asymmetry and thus substantially reduces the adverse secular drift in the model. In qualitative terms, the results of the revised model remain broadly similar: the US external accounts are on a path that involves a persistent, uncomfortably high deficit.

2. The rates used in the forecasts here are 84.3 yen per dollar and 1.41 deutsche marks per dollar. By late April the dollar had fallen even further against the two key currencies. Then by mid-August the dollar was back up sharply to 97 yen and 1.48 deutsche marks.

quarter of 1995 from the 1994 level, because real appreciation against the Mexican peso offset real depreciation against Pacific NIC and South American currencies.

For Japan, the RFM forecast through 1997 shows more favorable results: a substantial adjustment bringing the current account surplus down from $123 billion in 1994 (compared with an actual figure of $129 billion) to $87 billion by 1997. The EAG model shows the same 1997 outcome (although the model understates the 1994 surplus).

Although the forecasts show a major nominal deterioration in the US external accounts in 1995, they do not represent a correspondingly large drag on the US economy in real terms. The nominal deterioration of the current account by about $30 billion in 1995 (RFM2) is largely accounted for by changes in trade prices rather than in net import volume.[3]

The central question raised by the projections here, however, is whether the United States can responsibly, or even safely, accept a chronic current account deficit on the order of 2 percent of GDP (the 1997 rate if the deficit is $160 billion). One way to address this question is to consider what is the ceiling for a prudent steady-state ratio of net external debt to GDP, and then to see what is the ratio of the current account deficit to GDP that would cause the debt/GDP ratio to converge to this ceiling.

Net external debt is the cumulation of current account deficits. If nominal GDP is Y, real growth is at the rate g, inflation is at rate $\dot{p}$, and the current account deficit is a constant ratio μ of GDP, then in year t the ratio of external debt to GDP will be:

$$\frac{D_t}{Y_t} = \frac{\int_{t=0}^{t} \mu \, Y_0 \, e^{(g+\dot{p})\,t}}{Y_0 \, e^{(g+\dot{p})t}} = \frac{\mu}{g+\dot{p}} \qquad (23)$$

For the United States, real potential growth is usually placed at 2.5 percent, and inflation is likely to average 3 percent. From equation 23, this means that if the current account deficit is steady at 2 percent of GDP, the ratio of net external debt to GDP will converge to 36 percent (= .02/[.025 + .03]).

An external debt ratio of about 40 percent of GDP has typically been considered a threshold of danger for developing countries. For the 17

3. With a 7 percent rise in real import prices for industrial country goods, pass-through of 50 percent, and an import base of about $450 billion from industrial countries, price changes can account for the bulk of the change in net imports. This also means that the drag on the US economy from falling real net exports should be considerably less in 1995 than it was in the previous two years (−0.8 percent contribution to growth in 1993 and −0.7 percent in 1994; US Department of Commerce 1995c). The drag in 1995 should be −0.2 percent growth impact or less.

heavily indebted countries singled out in the Baker Plan of the mid-1980s, the ratio of net external debt to GDP stood at 41.5 percent in 1982 at the outbreak of the debt crisis (and rose as high as 67 percent in 1987; Cline 1995, 48).

Standard economic theory would suggest that ideally the United States should be a creditor rather than debtor country, because as a mature economy it is likely to have return on capital that is lower than that in emerging economies. On this basis, the United States should be running a current account surplus rather than a deficit.

Even limiting the analysis to what might be considered safe as opposed to what might be globally optimal, it is doubtful that the United States would be well advised to allow its debt/GDP ratio to climb to the threshold usually associated with debt difficulties. Because the US economy is so large relative to the world economy, it would seem more difficult for the country to mobilize the kind of continual borrowing that might be feasible on a proportional basis by smaller countries. The limits of prudence might thus suggest a ceiling debt ratio of perhaps half the usual threshold, or 20 percent of GDP. From equation 23, to limit the steady-state ratio of net external debt to GDP to 20 percent, it would be necessary to limit the annual current account deficit to 1.1 percent of GDP. The exercise here thus confirms the target suggested by Williamson (1985).

It would thus be risky to adopt a strategy of simply declaring victory on the current account deficit rather than seeking to reduce it. A target of 1.1 percent of GDP by 1997 would amount to a deficit of $88 billion. Instead, the central forecast for 1997 in table 5 is on the order of $160 billion. If we apply the RFM exchange rate impact parameter from table 6, in order to reduce the deficit to the target of $88 billion it would be necessary for the dollar to decline in real terms by an additional 5.7 percent (=[160-88]/12.6).

This policy diagnosis is diametrically opposed to the view that the dollar has fallen too far and, especially, that the Federal Reserve should push up interest rates in an effort to strengthen the dollar. Yet at the G-7 meeting of finance ministers in late April 1995, and again at the Halifax G-7 summit in mid-June 1995, officials of the Group of Seven industrial countries took the position that the dollar had fallen against the deutsche mark and yen by more than was justified by the fundamentals, and called for an "orderly reversal" (Group of Seven, 1995). As discussed below, in August 1995 intervention by the US, Japanese, and German central banks did indeed push the dollar higher, especially against the yen.

For the projections of this study to hold on course (especially for Japan), it will be necessary for the August 1995 recovery of the dollar against the yen and deutsche mark to be ephemeral, and for the yen to return to the range of 85 to the dollar and the deutsche mark to 1.4 to the dollar.

Assuming that the rates stabilize at their real levels of the second quarter of 1995, the large declines of the dollar against the yen and deutsche mark from 1994 to these levels do suggest that any further decline of the dollar on a trade-weighted basis should be accomplished primarily through appreciations against the dollar by other currencies, including several European currencies, the Canadian dollar, and currencies of the Pacific NICs.[4] Moreover, there should be some room for real appreciation of the Mexican peso by 1997 from second-quarter 1995 levels as more normal capital market conditions return.

China is one example of a developing country whose real exchange rate might appropriately appreciate. China had cumulative current account surpluses of $29 billion in 1990–92. Although its external balance slipped into a deficit of $12 billion in 1993 (as the economy overheated prior to restrictive measures), by 1994 an external surplus of about $10 billion or more had returned, and by the first quarter of 1995, exports had soared to more than 40 percent above imports. The combined influences of the return of current account surplus and massive capital inflows boosted the country's reserves from $23 billion in 1993 to $62 billion by the second quarter of 1995 (IMF 1995e).

Taiwan is another candidate for exchange rate appreciation. Although its current account surplus fell from an average of $11 billion annually in 1988–91 to $6 billion by 1994, the surplus remained at a sizable 2.2 percent of GDP, and reserves stood at $98 billion (Taiwan 1995). Singapore is another candidate, with a current account surplus of 4 percent of GDP. South Korea's case is less clear; the country already shifted from a current account surplus of $14 billion in 1988 to a deficit of $4.5 billion in 1994 (about 1 percent of GDP), but if a significant return to surplus developed, some real appreciation might also be appropriate for the Korean won.

---

4. Note that in Cline (1989, 228–29), a simulation of the EAG model for a Feasible Adjustment Program (FAP) called for an 11 percent real depreciation of the dollar from its fourth quarter 1987 level, reflecting a real appreciation of 28 percent for the yen, 23 percent for the deutsche mark, and lesser amounts for other European countries. The objective of the package was to bring the US current account deficit down to 1 percent of GDP while not imposing current account deficits in excess of 10 percent of exports on trade partners such as Canada and Italy.

It turns out that for the entire period 1988–94, the average real value of the dollar was only 3.8 percent below the post-Plaza low (which actually occurred in the second quarter of 1988, according to the IMF's REER). By mid-April 1995 the REER for the dollar was down by 12.5 percent from that earlier low. However, the delay in the adjustment, coupled with the possibly larger adverse secular drift in the US accounts than incorporated in the EAG parameters, means that by now the earlier proposed correction is insufficient.

As for the yen, the REER has risen by 37 percent from fourth quarter 1987, a larger adjustment than originally called for (but only after delay and movement in the wrong direction in 1988–89). The real rate reached by Germany in March 1995 was still about 10 percent below the level that would have resulted from application of the FAP proposal. However, in the meantime German reunification had brought a shock to the German external accounts that meant a lower current account position for a given real exchange rate.

A differentiated policy along these lines would make it possible to observe "speed limits" on any move of the dollar against the two other currencies that are key for international monetary purposes: the deutsche mark and the yen. Despite the relative magnitudes involved in the trade-off between growth and the exchange rate as analyzed below, the sharp rise of the yen in early 1995 no doubt did reduce the short-term prospects for recovery in the Japanese economy. Moreover, although the prospects remain strong for the dollar to retain its key-currency role (Frankel 1995), there are potential systemic risks from a rapid decline of the dollar against the deutsche mark and yen that are not present when the decline instead is against other, noncentral currencies that appreciate against the three key currencies.

While it is appropriate to observe speed limits, it is questionable whether the vehicle should suddenly be thrown into reverse. The strong rebound of the dollar against the yen and deutsche mark by mid-August 1995 would likely prove counterproductive if it were anything more than transitory.

The conclusion that the dollar had gone far enough against the yen (before the reversal by the third quarter of 1995) is supported by the projections for Japan's external balance. At the rate of 84 yen per dollar used in the analysis of this study, the Japanese external account was headed toward correction that would leave the surplus at about 1.4 percent of GDP, which would have been considered an acceptable level within the context of past US-Japanese policy discussions.[5]

The issue of whether and how much to support the dollar also involves behavior of domestic financial markets. Through mid-1995 the stock and bond markets were little affected by the dollar's decline. There was some risk that at some point the security markets could fall sharply because of an actual or anticipated rise in US interest rates provoked by a need to defend the dollar.

Indeed, the classic symptom of a "hard landing" is the coexistence of rising interest rates and a falling currency. This combination would mean that the supply curve of foreign capital is moving adversely because with an unchanged supply curve higher interest rates would instead bid up capital inflows and the price of the dollar. The outcome of the hard-landing scenario is sharply higher interest rates and an increase in the likelihood of a recession. A major reason not to try to push the dollar back up to 1994 levels is that the resulting increase in the external deficit by 1996–97 (to a level as high as $210 billion, as discussed above) could

5. In the "framework" trade negotiations with Japan, the Clinton administration indicated a range of 1 to 2 percent of GDP as the target that Japan should accept (Bergsten and Noland 1993, 208). Note, however, that the moderation of Japan's external surplus from its 1993 level of 3 percent of GDP is partly attributable to the major appreciation of the yen, which means that Japan's GDP should rise from $4.2 trillion in 1993 to $6.3 trillion by 1997.

Figure 16 United States: bilateral trade balances, 1980–94

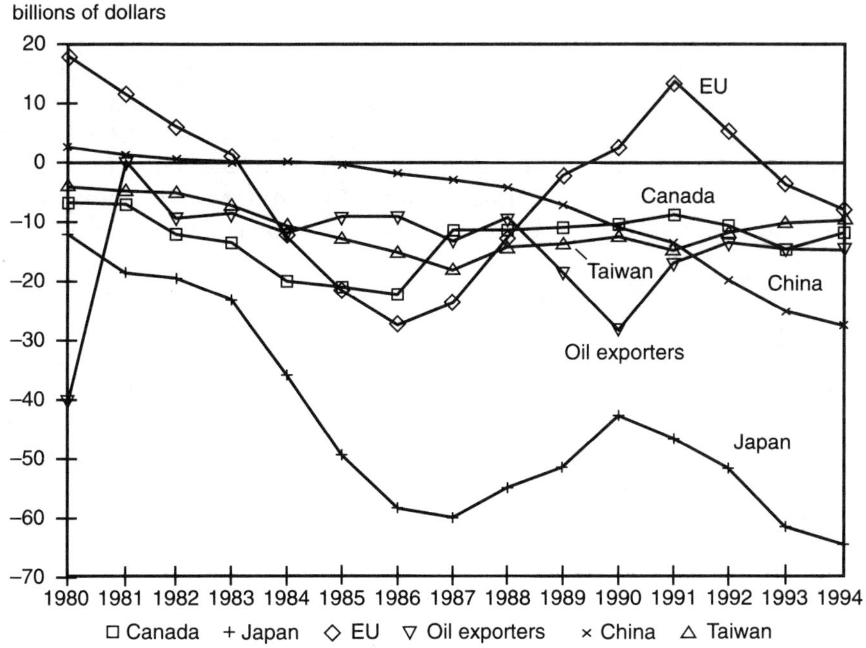

greatly increase the probability of an eventual hard landing. The same is largely true of the risk involved if the August 1995 dollar rally is anything more than transitory.

Another implication of these results may be the need for closer attention to trade trends with emerging market countries. The real exchange rate for US trade with LDCs may not fully capture trends in trade with such countries as China. Figure 16 shows the US bilateral balance with each of the six largest partners in terms of bilateral contribution to the overall US deficit. Aside from highlighting the well-known case of the large US deficit with Japan, the figure shows a sizable adverse trend in trade with China. It also suggests that for US overall trade to be closer in balance—for example, at the 1990 levels—the United States may need to run at least a modest structural surplus with the European Union.

Fiscal Adjustment

For US macroeconomic policy, the principal implication of this analysis is the need for further fiscal adjustment. Reducing the fiscal deficit should help reduce US interest rates, which in turn should allow the dollar to ease. Ironically, reducing the deficit should simultaneously help reduce the risk of a severe further plunge of the dollar.

Figure 17 shows the two alternative ways in which the fiscal deficit affects the dollar. In panel A, the demand (D) for foreign capital inflow (K) intersects the supply (S) at the initial interest rate (i_0). Then fiscal adjustment shifts the demand curve for foreign capital downward to the left. The new equilibrium interest rate is lower, at i_1. On the left side of the diagram, the real value of the dollar (expressed as DM/$) is higher when US interest rates are higher and thus more attractive to foreign capital. After fiscal adjustment, and at a lower interest rate, the equilibrium exchange rate is at fewer deutsche marks per dollar (i.e., a lower value of the dollar).

The usual relationship between the fiscal deficit and the dollar as mapped out in panel A of figure 17 is thus that fiscal contraction weakens the dollar. In this way, fiscal adjustment sets the stage for external adjustment even if there is no slowdown in growth (because "crowding in" of investment and higher exports replace demand previously coming from the fiscal deficit). On average, a $1 reduction in the fiscal deficit has been associated with a 50-cent reduction in the external deficit.[6]

However, the key to this mechanism is movement along an unchanged supply curve for foreign exchange. This amounts to an unchanged willingness of foreigners to acquire dollars in exchange for their currencies. Panel B shows the alternative situation in which changes in foreign investors' confidence can alter this foreign willingness to provide their currency in exchange for dollars.

This time the diagram shows supply and demand of dollars in the foreign exchange market at alternative prices of deutsche marks per dollar. Here the willingness of foreigners to acquire dollars is shown by the demand curve, D.[7] As shown in panel B, if foreign creditors become disheartened because of severe doubts about the longer-term stability of the US economy in the face of chronic fiscal and external deficits, their demand curve may shift backward to the left (from D to D'), as in the hard-landing scenario. The result will be a sharp depreciation of the dollar (from R_0 to R_1). There may have been an element of this dynamic at work in early 1995 (including at the moment of the defeat of the balanced budget amendment, and perhaps in part as a reaction to the reminder from the Mexican peso crisis that countries with large current account deficits can get into trouble).

If instead foreign creditors learn new information that improves their confidence about longer-term prospects, they may be prepared to extend

---

6. Helliwell (1991). However, care must be used to refer to the full-employment fiscal deficit when considering this relationship. In contrast, during a recession there is likely to be a negative relationship between changes in the fiscal and external deficits, because imports will be declining even as the fiscal deficit is rising as a consequence of falling tax revenue.

7. Foreigners' demand for dollars, curve D in panel B, is the same thing as foreigners' supply of foreign currency, curve S in panel A.

Figure 17 Fiscal adjustment, expectations, and the exchange rate

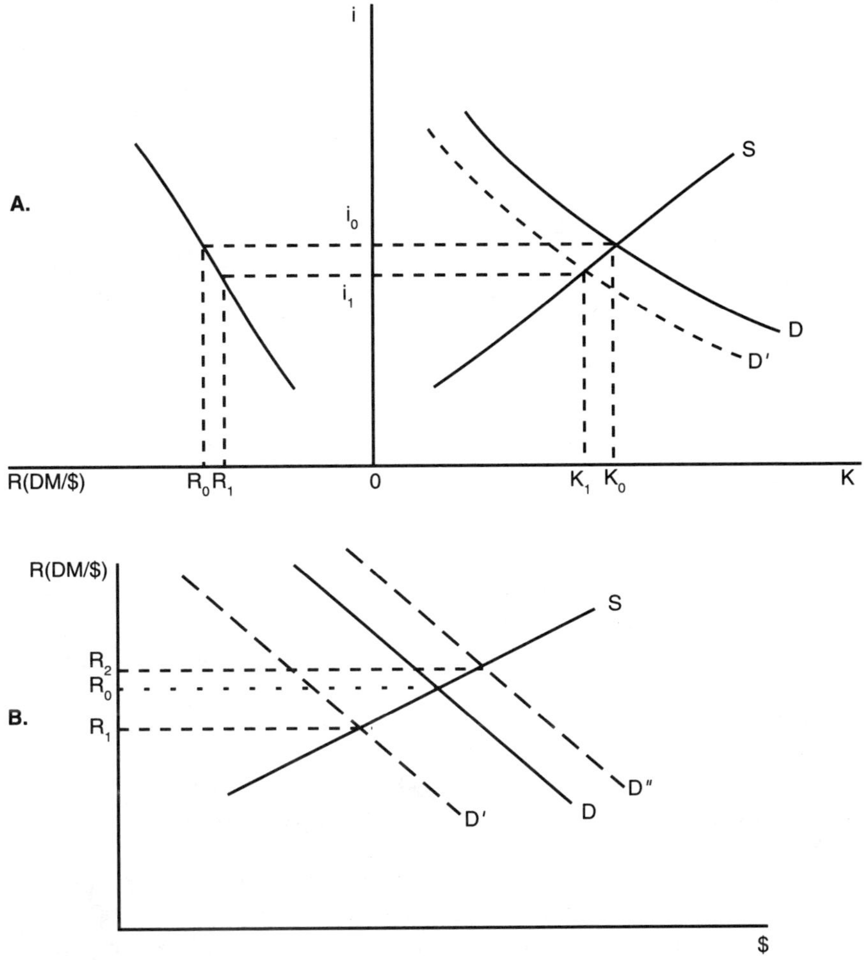

a larger amount of capital inflow at any given exchange rate, shifting the demand curve for dollars from D to D″ and strengthening the equilibrium exchange rate to R_2. Ironically, then, shifting toward a more sustainable fiscal path can help keep the dollar from collapsing (by avoiding an eventual wrenching shift from D to D′), and the announcement of a fiscal adjustment program may even temporarily strengthen the dollar (a shift to D″). In the latter case, however, the eventual accumulation of a larger current account deficit is likely to cause the currency to decline again.

Fiscal adjustment can help the US external accounts not only by permitting some further ease of the real dollar (figure 17, panel A) while limiting the risk of a serious further collapse (figure 17, panel B curve D′). In

Figure 18 Fiscal and current account deficits

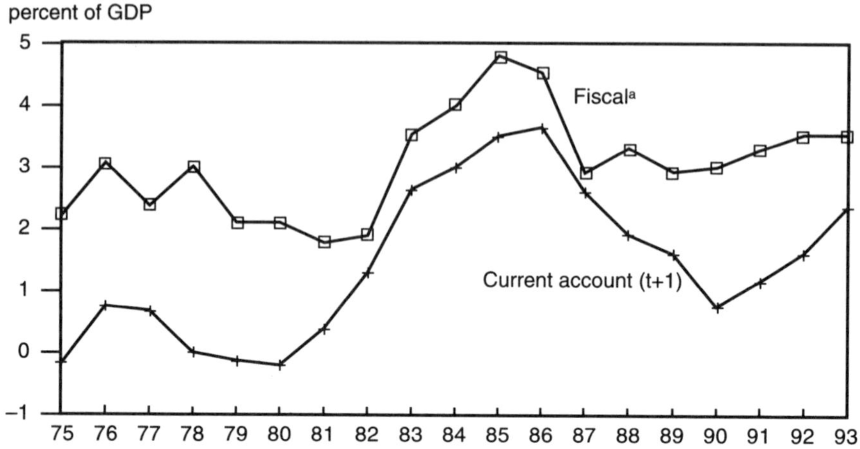

a. Standardized employment basis.

addition, with the lower interest rates resulting from fiscal adjustment, the factor services deficit will not be as large for any given stock of net external debt. As discussed above, the US balance on factor (capital) services has fallen to zero from a surplus of nearly $40 billion in 1981, and this balance is likely to be in deficit by over $20 billion by 1997 (figure 11 and table 2). As an approximation, this balance equals gross US foreign assets multiplied by the foreign interest rate, less gross US debt to foreigners multiplied by the US interest rate. The difference can thus be quite sensitive to a reduction in US interest rates.

In sum, US fiscal adjustment is the key underlying policy for external adjustment. It is thus encouraging that in mid-1995 the US Congress adopted a goal of eliminating the fiscal deficit by 2002.[8] In contrast, the baseline outlook as of January 1995 had called for a deficit of $224 billion by 1997 and $243 billion by 2000 (CBO 1995, xvi).

Figure 18 supports the idea that reducing the fiscal deficit will reduce the current account deficit. The figure shows the "standardized employment" deficit as a percentage of GDP (CBO 1995, 91). This measure corrects for cyclical effects on the deficit and also removes the influence of the savings and loan bailout expenses as well as the fiscal receipts from other nations in support of US operations in the Gulf War (mainly in 1991). The current account deficit as a percentage of GDP is also shown in the figure, but for the subsequent year. The current account deficit for 1991 (i.e., shown

8. The budget resolution called for the deficit to fall from $175 billion in 1995 to $170 billion in 1996, $152 billion in 1997, $116 billion in 1998, $100 billion in 1999, $80 billion in 2000, and $33 billion by 2001, reaching a surplus of $6 billion in 2002 (US Congress 1995, 44).

as 1990 in figure 18) is adjusted upward by $40 billion to take account of unusual transfers from the Gulf War.

A relationship between the standardized employment deficit and the current account deficit in the subsequent year is evident in figure 18. A simple statistical regression in fact shows a highly significant relationship between the two and indeed shows that the coefficient on the fiscal deficit is greater than unity.[9]

On a basis of the 50 percent rule of thumb noted above (Helliwell 1991), elimination of a fiscal deficit of 2.8 percent of GDP (the 1994 level, standardized employment basis) could be expected to reduce the current account deficit by 1.4 percent of GDP. The forecasts here indicate a baseline external deficit of 2 percent of GDP by 1997 (assuming prompt return to the real exchange rates of second quarter 1995). With secular drift ranging from −$6 billion annually (0.1 percent of GDP) to −$22 billion annually (0.3 percent of GDP; table 6), by 2002 the baseline external deficit could thus range from 2.5 to 3.5 percent of GDP in the absence of fiscal adjustment. The proposed elimination of the deficit could thus reduce the external deficit in 2002 to between 1.1 and 2.1 percent of GDP, using the 50 percent rule. If the more striking coefficient of nearly unity found in the simple regression here is applied, the implied current account balance by 2002 would stand in a range of a *surplus* of 0.3 percent of GDP to a deficit of 0.7 percent.

In broad terms, elimination of the fiscal deficit would be likely to successfully bring the US external deficit within the target range of 1 percent of GDP or lower. There is thus a major side benefit of fiscal adjustment that has received little attention in the 1995 policy discussions: fiscal correction would deal with the problem of excessive external deficit and growing indebtedness to the rest of the world, in addition to addressing the domestic economic problems of pressure on interest rates and imposition of a burden on taxpayers in the future.

Two further aspects of the fiscal–external adjustment link warrant attention. First, there is the question of the extent to which fiscal adjustment will translate into slower domestic growth because of Keynesian demand contraction. The prevailing current view is that most of any such contraction can be offset by the stimulus from lower interest rates made possible by the fiscal correction. However, it should be kept in mind that if there is a boost to domestic investment (or interest-sensitive consumption) from this source, the adjustment in the external accounts will be attenuated.

9. The regression is: $c_t = -2.26 + 1.21 f_{t-1}; \bar{R}^2 = 0.72$

$$\quad\quad\quad (0.72) \quad (0.20)$$

where c is the current account deficit as a percentage of GDP, f is the standardized employment fiscal deficit as a percentage of GDP, and standard errors are in parentheses. A similar regression using contemporaneous rather than lagged fiscal deficits yields a similar coefficient (1.17) but a lower degree of explanation ($\bar{R}^2 = 0.53$).

That is, from the accounting identity whereby the external deficit equals the difference between investment and saving and to the extent that greater private investment replaces less government deficit spending, the result will be favorable for growth but unfavorable for external adjustment (because the reduction in government dissaving will be offset by increased private investment).[10]

Second, the timing of fiscal correction will be important. There is a strong political temptation to concentrate adjustment at distant dates. The path in the congressional budget resolution discussed above does this; it cuts the deficit by $59 billion in the first three years and by an additional $122 billion over the next four years.[11] It will be important to keep the fiscal adjustment path as front-loaded as is politically feasible because otherwise the cumulative increase in external debt from ongoing current account deficits will be large, with implications for future external payments on capital services.

The Guns of August: Dollar Redux?

Whereas US fiscal deliberations by mid-1995 gave grounds for hope that the US external deficit could be brought down to an acceptable level within a horizon of seven years, US exchange rate policy by the third quarter of 1995 provided grounds for serious concern about further pressure for external disequilibrium within a horizon of two to three years. The United States and Japan put teeth in the G-7 call for dollar reversal in early August 1995, when monetary authorities of the two countries intervened jointly to push up the dollar against the yen. The move coincided with the Japanese government's announcement of moves to liberalize capital outflows through foreign investments of insurance companies and to encourage government entities to invest abroad (*New York Times*, 2 August 1995). The result was a gratifying (to the authorities) jump in the yen (which had already drifted to 88 to the dollar by the end of July) to nearly 91 to the dollar. The question was whether the instrument of coordinated exchange market intervention was pointed in the right direction. Then on 15 August, joint intervention by the central banks of the United States, Germany, and Japan helped push up the dollar further, to 97 yen and 1.48 deutsche marks (*New York Times*, 16 August 1995).

---

10. Translating fiscal correction to external correction will correspondingly be more successful if there is a greater rather than lesser exchange rate effect, which will tend to push the composition of demand change toward increased net exports rather than increased domestic private consumption and investment to replace reduced government deficits. For a discussion of the importance of exchange rate change in facilitating external adjustment as the consequence of fiscal adjustment, see Krugman (1991b).

11. To a modest extent, back-end loading is inherent because of the cumulative effect of savings on interest on government debt.

The case for boosting the dollar significantly against even the yen would have to require either a lack of concern about the large Japanese surplus and large US external deficit, or an overriding concern about economic unraveling in Japan if the yen does not weaken. Some might argue that the strong yen depresses the Japanese economy so much that Japan's current account surplus has a positive sign with respect to the strength of the yen. That argument would be difficult to sustain from the model estimates here. As shown in table 6, each percent rise in the real yen generates a reduction in the external surplus of at least $2 billion. As discussed below, the 12 percent trade-weighted real depreciation of the yen from April 1995 to 15 August could thus frustrate some $25 billion of the prospective correction in the Japanese surplus by 1997 projected in table 5. At a parameter of about $3 billion (RFM) per percentage point of growth (table 6), Japan's growth rate would need to rise by about 8 percentage-point-years to neutralize the current account effects of the weakening of the yen from second quarter 1995 to August. Yet it would require an extreme mechanism to generate 8 percentage points of Japanese GDP growth—worth about $400 billion—from a cumulative increment of only about $37 billion in the trade balance over 1996–97 (i.e., the 1997 increment plus the 1996 phase-in). Macroeconomic multipliers of ten-to-one should be suspect.

Extreme stories might arguably be told, centered around the weak banking industry, for example. Just conceivably, a weaker yen could alleviate balance-sheet pressure so that banks would resume lending and spark the moribund Japanese economy. Or, just conceivably, Japanese business and consumer psychology is so fixated on the yen that investment and consumption would rise disproportionately from a weakening of the yen. Such mechanisms, however, would likely generate far less than a $400 billion GDP gain as the consequence of the possible trade balance swing purchased with a 12 percent yen depreciation.

Moreover, an attempt by Japanese (and G-7) authorities to revive the Japanese economy through yen reversal would mean a failure to come to grips with the more fundamental problem: the need to replace external demand with domestic demand. Until the Japanese economy makes the transition from exports to domestic demand as the engine of growth, there will be a persistent incompatibility between more moderate Japanese external surpluses and revival of the Japanese economy.

Despite the dubious case for pushing the dollar back up, central bank intervention in the first two weeks of August 1995 succeeded in driving the currency to 97 yen and 1.48 deutsche marks. The intervention was "leaning with the wind," as the dollar was moving up against the yen already in the market. The effect was to cause a considerable depreciation of the dollar against the April 1995 levels used for the baseline analysis of this study. Against that benchmark, by 15 August the dollar had risen by 15 percent against the yen and the deutsche mark, 10 percent against the Swiss franc, and about 3 to 5 percent against currencies of France, the Netherlands, Belgium, Denmark, Norway, Portugal, and Austria. However, the dollar had fallen by 1.4 percent against the key Canadian dollar (and by 6 percent against the erratic Italian lira). On a trade-weighted basis against 18 industrial country currencies, the dollar rose by 4 percent from the April benchmark.

Although the Dallas Federal Reserve estimates for LDC exchange rates were not available as this study went to press, a reasonable guess would be that the dollar rose about 1 percent against these currencies from the April 1995 base used in this study. Overall the trade-weighted rise of the dollar would have thus been 2.8 percent. Applying the RFM impact parameter from table 6 of $12.6 billion per percent on the real exchange rate, the result would be that if the rates of mid-August were to persist, the 1997 US current account deficit would be $35 billion larger than in the baseline (table 5). On this basis, the RFM1 would place the 1997 deficit at $197 billion.

In sum, as G-7 authorities congratulated themselves on their success in reviving the dollar and bringing down the deutsche mark and especially the yen, they set the stage for widening the external imbalances in the future. With the two-year lag from exchange rates to trade performance, the chickens would only come home to roost at a date safely past the US presidential elections of November 1996, and in the meantime officials could emphasize the merits of reduced inflationary pressure from a stronger dollar and greater assurance that the Federal Reserve would not need to push up interest rates to defend the dollar. It remained to be seen, most importantly, whether the dollar's revival would stand the test of time. It was also unclear whether the politics involved were as benign as might have been assumed. US manufacturing jobs were likely to be affected adversely by the eventual outcome.[12]

The August 1995 reversal of the dollar meant that the 7 percent real decline against industrial country currencies from the 1994 level turned into a decline of only 3 percent; and the trade-weighted change including LDCs correspondingly changed from a 4 percent reduction to a decline of only about 1.2 percent. However, these reversals were small compared to that for the yen. The real value of the yen against 18 industrial country currencies depreciated by 12 percent from April 1995 to mid-August. Applying the RFM impact parameter of table 5, the implication was that Japan's 1997 current account surplus would be $25 billion larger than in the baseline, standing at $112 billion. Thus, the lift to investor spirits in

12. Borjas and Ramey (1994) present provocative evidence that an important factor in the rise of inequality between college- and high school–educated workers in the late 1980s was the deterioration in the US trade balance in consumer durable manufactures, and thus the weakening of union power to extract wage rents in these sectors. The trade deterioration was the consequence of the overvalued dollar in the mid-1980s.

Japan from the yen's return to levels close to those of 1994 was likely to come at the cost of future US-Japan trade tension as a consequence of a much more meager reduction in the Japanese external surplus.

Nonetheless, there was a considerable likelihood that the central banks' guns of August would prove no match for the eventual market logic that countries with enormous trade deficits tend to experience exchange rate depreciations against the currencies of those with enormous trade surpluses. In that case, the baseline exchange rates and current account projections of this study would remain more relevant than the parametrically altered forecasts just discussed.

Overview

The salient findings of this study (in addition to its introduction of a new, streamlined model for the current account) include the following.

First, there are underlying economic reasons that can explain the decline of the dollar in the first half of 1995, and this decline was not merely an aberrant whim of financial markets. Namely, the US current account deficit is not only large but is on a path toward substantial increase in 1995 and only meager correction thereafter. Indeed, if real exchange rates had remained unchanged at their 1994 levels, the United States would have been headed for a current account deficit of about $210 billion by 1997 (chapter 3).

Second, a policy corollary is that it would be a mistake to take forceful measures of intervention and tightening of monetary policy in an attempt to boost the dollar back up to 1994 levels. US monetary policy should continue to address primarily domestic considerations, unless the dollar slides to much lower levels. As for intervention, the G-7 efforts, especially in August 1995, seem likely to prove to be a mistake that aggravates external imbalances.

Third, the decline of the dollar was much smaller than generally recognized. Although the dollar fell by 17.5 percent against the yen and 13 percent against the deutsche mark from the 1994 average to the second-quarter 1995 levels, it was only down about 7 percent against industrial country currencies overall and down only about 4 percent on a comprehensive trade-weighted basis that includes developing country currencies. By the second quarter of 1995, the dollar was unchanged from the 1994 average real level against currencies of developing-countries, because the large increase against the Mexican peso offset decreases against Pacific NIC and South American currencies.

Fourth, despite the decline of the dollar in the first half of 1995, there is likely to be a sharp deterioration of the US current account deficit in 1995.[13] The deficit is likely to rise from $156 billion last year to the range

13. In fact the decline may actually contribute to the 1995 deficit through the J-curve effect.

of $180 billion to $200 billion in 1995. By 1996–97 the deficit is likely to remain in the vicinity of $160 billion if the dollar stabilizes at its real level of second quarter 1995. The surge this year is partly driven by the rise of the dollar in 1993 because there is a two-year lag from the exchange rate signal to the trade outcome. In addition, the deterioration reflects the effects of the Mexican peso crisis, and the annual worsening of the capital services balance from growing external debt. The 1995 deterioration should not exert a major drag on domestic growth, because much of the effect is from trade prices rather than volumes.

Fifth, the foremost policy measure for dealing with the external deficit should be further reduction of the fiscal deficit. Lower interest rates resulting from fiscal correction can directly help reduce the widening deficit on capital services and can indirectly induce further easing of the dollar and increased competitiveness. If the United States succeeds in meeting the congressional target of eliminating the budget deficit by 2002, the US current account deficit would probably fall to 1 percent of GDP or below. However, the budget plan is concentrated in the later years of this horizon.

Sixth, if the United States is to limit its long-term ratio of net external debt to GDP to a safe range of 20 percent or less, it will be necessary to cut the current account deficit to about 1 percent of GDP, or half the projected 1997 level. To obtain this outcome, it is likely to be necessary for the dollar to decline further by about 5 percent from the second quarter 1995 levels on a trade-weighted basis.

Seventh, the Japanese yen had risen by so much that it would have been inappropriate to seek further decline of the dollar against the yen (beyond the level of 84 to the dollar used in the projections of this study). The rise in the yen had already set Japan on course for reduction of its external surplus to slightly below $90 billion by 1997 (1.4 percent of GDP), and the steep decline in 1995 had clouded prospects for recovery of the Japanese economy. Even so, the obverse does not seem warranted either, and the joint US-Japanese intervention in August 1995 that helped push the dollar back to 97 yen by midmonth seemed questionable at best and more likely ill-advised. The results of this study indicate that instead the yen should go back to about 85 to the dollar.

Eighth, the corresponding implication is that there might need to be further real dollar depreciation in the range of, say, 6 to 10 percent against a wider array of other currencies, including those of the NICs.

Ninth, "speed limit" considerations would have made it undesirable for there to be much further depreciation of the dollar in mid-1995 even against the deutsche mark and some other European currencies. However, the joint intervention that pushed the dollar up briskly against the yen and deutsche mark in August 1995 was a policy mistake that could prove costly to adjustment unless the dollar reversal turns out to be merely transitory.

Appendix

Technical Note 1: Elasticity of Supply

As discussed in chapter 2, the single-equation estimates of this study assume infinitely elastic supply of imports and exports, so that the estimated price coefficient represents a demand elasticity. It is "customary" to assume that import supply is infinitely elastic (e.g., Noland 1989). Even for the United States, which as the world's largest importer would be the most likely to face an upward sloping (finite elasticity) import supply curve, imports account for only 18 percent of world exports (excluding US exports; GATT 1994, 8). Thus, to increase US imports by 10 percent requires an increase of export supply from the rest of the world by less than 2 percent, a magnitude sufficiently small to be unlikely to require a major increase in marginal costs of foreign producers. For Japan, the assumption of infinitely elastic import supply should be even more realistic, because Japan imports only 7 percent of world exports.

On the export side, in contrast, there is usually more concern about noninfinitely elastic supply, and hence about the need to apply simultaneous-equation estimates (Goldstein and Kahn 1985). However, most countries have much higher ratios of exports to GDP than either the United States (10 percent for goods and nonfactor services in 1994) or Japan (9.4 percent in 1993; IMF 1995d). The lesser openness of these two economies primarily reflects the fact that they are the two largest economies in the world, and there is a well-known inverse relationship between size of the economy and share of external trade in the economy (e.g., Bergsten and Cline 1985, 75). Because of the relatively low export shares in GDP (and even taking into account the distinction between the base of tradeable goods and total GDP), for the United States and Japan the assumption of infinitely elastic export supply should not be a serious exaggeration. That is, even relatively large proportionate increases in the export quantity represent small proportionate increases in domestic production under these circumstances.

However, it should be kept in mind that if export supply is less than infinitely elastic, the single-equation estimates here will tend to understate demand elasticities.[1] This might be a problem if the estimated elasticities were low. However, as discussed in chapter 2, the estimates here show relatively brisk response of trade to prices.

Technical Note 2: Pass-Through Estimates

As noted in chapter 2, the estimates in table 1 of coefficients on the lagged nominal exchange rate (π_2) and on the current nominal exchange rate (π_5) contain combinations of the underlying pass-through ratios for import prices (ρ) and for export prices (ε), as well as an intermixture with the direct price elasticities for imports (ϕ) and exports (β). More specifically:

$$\pi_2 = -[\phi(1+\rho) + \beta\varepsilon], \text{ and } \pi_5 = \rho\text{-}\varepsilon$$

The estimated parameter $\pi_1 = \phi\text{-}\beta$ provides a third relationship. In principle, imposing some plausible relationship between the two trade price elasticities ϕ and β would provide a fourth relationship necessary to solve for the four unknowns.

---

1. Consider a supply-demand diagram for US exports, depicted from the viewpoint of the foreign purchaser. The US export supply curve is assumed to be horizontal. Depreciation of the dollar by 10 percent simply lowers this supply line uniformly by 10 percent in terms of the foreign currency price paid by the customer. The new trade equilibrium occurs downward to the right moving along the foreign demand curve for US exports. The estimated elasticity equals the observed percentage increase in export quantity divided by the 10 percent price change.

Now consider the same diagram with the same initial price-quantity equilibrium, but with an upward sloping supply curve for US exports. The 10 percent depreciation now shifts this curve downward everywhere by 10 percent (from the foreign viewpoint). As foreigners move downward to the right along their demand curve and the quantity of US exports increases, the supply price increases (because of less than infinitely elastic supply). The resulting equilibrium involves a smaller increase in quantity exported. It also involves a net reduction in price facing the foreigner of less than 10 percent because the effect of the downward shift in the supply curve was partly frustrated by upward movement toward the right along the new supply curve. With a smaller percentage change in quantity divided by the same (but now mistakenly imputed) 10 percent price change, the estimate of the price elasticity of foreign demand will now be understated.

It turns out that the estimated coefficients π_2 and π_5 in the US equation A (table 1) are incompatible with plausible and consistent values of ρ, ε, ϕ, and β.[2] However, the two estimated coefficients are not statistically significant. Nor are they significantly different in statistical terms from alternative values that in fact would be consistent with plausible pass-through ratios.[3] One set of pass-through ratios that meets this condition (import pass-through of 50 percent, export pass-through of 63 percent; see the preceding note) is only moderately lower than the values estimated by Hooper and Marquez (1995) for the United States (55 percent pass-through for imports and 84 percent for exports).[4] For Japan also, the direct estimates of the parameters that contain the pass-through ratios (π_2 and π_5) are not particularly compatible with plausible values. Hooper and Marquez (1995) estimate that import pass-through for Japan is almost complete ($\rho \approx -1$) and that export pass-through is about 85 percent ($\varepsilon = -0.15$). The difference far exceeds that in the equation estimated here ($\pi_5 = \rho\text{-}\varepsilon = -.26$; table 1). Yet if reasonable pass-through estimates

2. In iterations of 10 different combinations of ϕ (ranging from $\phi = \pi_1$, $\beta = 0$ to $\phi = 0$, $\beta = -\pi_1$) and 10 different values of ρ (from -1 to 0) and corresponding values of $\varepsilon = \rho - \pi_5$, the resulting array of 100 combinations shows only two that generate a value for $-[\phi(1+\rho)+\beta\varepsilon]$ that is close to the estimated value of $\pi_2 = -0.183$; and both have extreme properties ($\beta=0$, $\varepsilon=-.833$ in one case; $\phi = 0.0827$, $\rho = -0.1$, in the other).

3. When the import pass-through ratio is set at 50 percent ($\rho = -0.5$), the highest export pass-through ratio that is compatible with the estimated coefficient $\pi_5 = 0.033$ not being statistically different from the alternative hypothesized value at the 10 percent level is $\varepsilon = -0.37$, meaning 63 percent pass-through of the exchange rate to export prices (and implying the alternative $\pi_5' = -0.13$). Similarly, with these pass-through values, if it is further assumed that $\phi = |\beta| = \pi_1/2$, then the resulting hypothesized value for π_2 becomes -0.36. The measured value of π_2 is not significantly different from this alternative hypothesized value.

That is, with the estimated $\pi_5 = \rho\text{-}\varepsilon = 0.033$ and a standard error of 0.0999, and the threshold t statistic of 1.64 for significance at the 10 percent level, if we set $\rho = -0.5$ and solve for ε in: $[0.033-(-0.5-\varepsilon)]/0.0999 \leq 1.64$, we have $\varepsilon \leq -0.369$, with the corresponding "prior value" estimate of $\pi_5' = -0.131$. Dividing the import and export price elasticities evenly so that $\phi = |\beta| = \pi_2/2$, and applying $\pi_2 = -[\phi(1+\rho)+\beta\varepsilon]$, we have the corresponding "prior value" estimate of $\pi_2' = -[0.4135(0.5) + -0.4135(-0.369)] = -0.36$. The t statistic for difference of this prior value from the estimate in table 1, with a standard error of 0.413 for this estimate, is: $[-0.183 - (-0.36)]/0.413 = 0.43$, too low for statistical significance at the 10 percent level.

4. Note, moreover, that the pass-through estimates here are for US trade with industrial countries. If the assumption here is correct, that US exporters feel that conditions of competitive pressure force them to absorb part of any real exchange rate appreciation rather than pass the entire change along in prices expressed in foreign currency, but that they feel no similar pressure for sales to developing countries, one would expect the export price pass-through for total US trade (the equations estimated by Hooper and Marquez) to be higher than that for trade with industrial countries only. Similarly, if LDC exporters feel they are not in a position to increase their profit margins rather than pass through price changes when their real exchange rates depreciate relative to the dollar, the weighted overall pass-through ratio for US imports should be higher than the corresponding ratio for US imports from industrial countries.

with the estimated difference are selected (for example, $\rho = -.63$, $\varepsilon = -.37$, for 63 percent pass-through on both sides), the implied value of the other relevant parameter (π_2) is substantially different from the estimated value.[5]

Once again, however, it is possible to specify plausible pass-through ratios for Japan that turn out not to differ significantly, in statistical terms, from the relevant estimated parameters. If we follow Hooper and Marquez (1995) and place a relatively high pass-through ratio on imports of 80 percent and then calculate the export pass-through ratio that is as high as possible without causing the resulting prior value of π_5 to differ significantly at the 10 percent level from the parameter estimated in table 1, it turns out that the resulting export pass-through is a plausible 71 percent.[6]

---

5. Again combining alternative values of the import and export price elasticities to sum to the observed parameter π_1, and applying alternative combinations of the pass-through parameters that yield the estimated value of $\pi_5 = -.26$, for the 10 (of 100 possible) combinations that place the pass-through ratios in the desired range (about 60 to 65 percent on both sides), the resulting value for π_2 lies in the range -0.7 to -0.8, whereas the estimated value is -1.03 (table 1).

6. Following note 5, with estimated $\pi_5 = \rho - \varepsilon = -0.26$, standard error of 0.151, and hypothesized $\rho = -0.8$; from $[-0.26-(-0.8-\varepsilon)]/0.151 \leq 1.64$, we have $\varepsilon \leq -0.292$, and $\pi_5' = -0.508$. Again dividing the import and export price elasticities evenly, we have $\pi_2' = -[0.9945(0.2) + -0.9945(-0.292)] = -0.489$. With standard error on the estimated $\pi_2 = 0.354$, the t statistic for difference from the hypothesized value is: $[-1.035 - (-0.489)]/0.354 = 1.54$, too low for statistical significance at the 10 percent level.

References

Bergsten, C. Fred, ed. 1991. *International Adjustment and Financing*. Washington: Institute for International Economics.

Bergsten, C. Fred, and William R. Cline. 1985. *The United States–Japan Economic Problem*. POLICY ANALYSES IN INTERNATIONAL ECONOMICS 13. Washington: Institute for International Economics.

Bergsten, C. Fred, and Marcus Noland. 1993. *Reconcilable Differences? United States–Japan Economic Conflict*. Washington: Institute for International Economics.

Blue Chip. 1995. *Blue Chip Economic Indicators* 20, no. 8 (10 August).

Borjas, George J., and Valerie A. Ramey. 1994. "The Relationship between Wage Inequality and International Trade." In J. H. Bergstrand, T. F. Cosimano, J. W. Houck, and R. G. Sheehan. *The Changing Distribution of Income in an Open U.S. Economy*. Amsterdam: North-Holland.

Bryant, Ralph C., Peter Hooper, and Catherine L. Mann, eds. 1993. *Evaluating Policy Regimes: New Research in Empirical Macroeconomics*. Washington: Brookings Institution.

Congressional Budget Office (CBO). 1995. *The Economic and Budget Outlook: Fiscal Years 1996–2000*. Washington (January).

Council of Economic Advisers (CEA). 1995. *Economic Report of the President*. Washington (February).

Cline, William R. 1989. *United States External Adjustment and the World Economy*. Washington: Institute for International Economics.

Cline, William R. 1991a. "The Dollar, the Budget, and US External Adjustment." Washington: Institute for International Economics. Photocopy.

Cline, William R. 1991b. "US External Adjustment: Progress, Prognosis, and Interpretation." In C. Fred Bergsten, *International Adjustment and Financing*. Washington: Institute for International Economics.

Cline, William R. 1993. "Macroeconomics and the US-Japan Trade Imbalance." *International Economic Insights* 4, no. 4 (July-August): 5–8.

Cline, William R. 1994. *International Economic Policy in the 1990s*. Cambridge, MA: MIT Press.

Cline, William R. 1995. *International Debt Reexamined*. Washington: Institute for International Economics.

Frankel, Jeffrey. 1995. "Still the Lingua Franca," *Foreign Affairs* 74, no. 4 (July/August): 9–16.

General Agreement on Tariffs and Trade (GATT). 1994. *International Trade: Trends and Statistics, 1994*. Geneva.

Goldstein, Morris, and Mohsin S. Khan. 1985. "Income and Price Effects in Foreign Trade." In Ronald W. Jones and Peter B. Kenen, *Handbook of International Economics*, vol. 2. Amsterdam: Elsevier.

Group of Seven. 1995. *Halifax Summit Communiqué*. Halifax (16 June).

Harvey, Andrew C. 1994. *Time Series Models*. 2nd ed. Cambridge, MA: MIT Press.

Helkie, William L., and Peter Hooper. 1988. "An Empirical Analysis of the External Deficit, 1980–86." In Ralph C. Bryant, Gerald Holtham, and Peter Hooper, *External Deficits and the Dollar: The Pit and the Pendulum*. Washington: Brookings Institution.

Helliwell, John F. 1991. "The Fiscal Deficit and the External Deficit: Siblings but Not Twins." In Rudolph G. Penner, *The Great Fiscal Experiment*. Washington: Urban Institute.

Hooper, Peter, and Jaime Marquez. 1995. "Exchange Rates, Prices, and External Adjustment." In Peter B. Kenen, *Understanding Interdependence: The Macroeconomics of the Open Economy*. Princeton: Princeton University Press.

Houthakker, Henry, and Stephen P. Magee. 1969. "Income and Price Elasticities in World Trade." *Review of Economics and Statistics* 51: 111–25.

International Monetary Fund (IMF). 1987. *World Economic Outlook*. Washington (October).

International Monetary Fund. 1994a. *World Economic Outlook*. Washington (October).

International Monetary Fund. 1994b. *International Financial Statistics Yearbook 1994*. Washington.

International Monetary Fund. 1994c. *Direction of Trade Yearbook*. Washington.

International Monetary Fund. 1995a. *International Financial Statistics*. Washington (March).

International Monetary Fund. 1995b. *Direction of Trade Statistics Quarterly*. Washington (March).

International Monetary Fund. 1995c. *World Economic Outlook*. Washington (May).

International Monetary Fund. 1995d. *International Financial Statistics*. Washington (June).

International Monetary Fund. 1995e. *International Finance Statistics*. Washington (August).

Krugman, Paul. 1991a. "Introduction." In C. Fred Bergsten, *International Adjustment and Financing*. Washington: Institute for International Economics.

Krugman, Paul R. 1991b. "Has the Adjustment Process Worked?" In C. Fred Bergsten, *International Adjustment and Financing*. Washington: Institute for International Economics.

Lawrence, Robert Z. 1990. "US Current Account Adjustment: An Appraisal." *Brookings Papers on Economic Activity*, no. 2: 343–83.

Marris, Stephen. 1985. *Deficits and the Dollar: The World Economy at Risk*. POLICY ANALYSES IN INTERNATIONAL ECONOMICS 14. Washington: Institute for International Economics.

Marquez, Jaime. 1993. "The Autonomy of Elasticities for Trade among Canada, Japan, and the United States." In *Japan and the World Economy*, vol. 5: 179–95.

Masson, P. R., S. Symansky, and G. Meredith. 1990. *MULTIMOD Mark II: A Revised and Extended Model*. Occasional Paper 71. Washington: International Monetary Fund.

Noland, Marcus. 1989. "Japanese Trade Elasticities and the J-Curve." *Review of Economics and Statistics* 71 (February): 175–79.

Prestowitz, Clyde V., Jr. 1988. *Trading Places: How America Allowed Japan to Take the Lead*. Tokyo: Charles E. Tuttle.

Taiwan, Central Bank of China. 1995. *Financial Statistics*. May.

US Congress, US House of Representatives. 1995. *Concurrent Resolution on the Budget for Fiscal Year 1996: Conference Report*. Report 104-159 (26 June).

US Department of Commerce. 1995a. "US International Trade in Goods and Services: December 1994." *Commerce News*, 17 February.

US Department of Commerce. 1995b."US International Transactions: Fourth Quarter and Year 1994." *Commerce News*, 14 March.

US Department of Commerce. 1995c. "US International Transactions: First Quarter 1995." Washington: Bureau of Economic Analysis, BEA 95-30 (21 June).

US Department of Commerce. 1995d. "Gross Domestic Product: First Quarter 1995 (Final)." Washington: Bureau of Economic Analysis (30 June).

US Department of Commerce. 1995e. "US International Trade in Goods and Services: June 1995." Washington: Bureau of Economic Analysis, FT-900: 95-06 (17 August).

Williamson, John. 1985. *The Exchange Rate System.* POLICY ANALYSES IN INTERNATIONAL ECONOMICS 5. Washington: Institute for International Economics.

Other Publications from the **Institute for International Economics**

POLICY ANALYSES IN INTERNATIONAL ECONOMICS Series

1 **The Lending Policies of the International Monetary Fund**
John Williamson/*August 1982*
ISBN paper 0-88132-000-5 72 pp.

2 **"Reciprocity": A New Approach to World Trade Policy?**
William R. Cline/*September 1982*
ISBN paper 0-88132-001-3 41 pp.

3 **Trade Policy in the 1980s**
C. Fred Bergsten and William R. Cline/*November 1982*
(out of print) ISBN paper 0-88132-002-1 84 pp.
Partially reproduced in the book *Trade Policy in the 1980s.*

4 **International Debt and the Stability of the World Economy**
William R. Cline/*September 1983*
ISBN paper 0-88132-010-2 134 pp.

5 **The Exchange Rate System, Second Edition**
John Williamson/*September 1983, rev. June 1985*
(out of print) ISBN paper 0-88132-034-X 61 pp.

6 **Economic Sanctions in Support of Foreign Policy Goals**
Gary Clyde Hufbauer and Jeffrey J. Schott/*October 1983*
ISBN paper 0-88132-014-5 109 pp.

7 **A New SDR Allocation?**
John Williamson/*March 1984*
ISBN paper 0-88132-028-5 61 pp.

8 **An International Standard for Monetary Stabilization**
Ronald I. McKinnon/*March 1984*
(out of print) ISBN paper 0-88132-018-8 108 pp.

9 **The Yen/Dollar Agreement: Liberalizing Japanese Capital Markets**
Jeffrey A. Frankel/*December 1984*
ISBN paper 0-88132-035-8 86 pp.

10 **Bank Lending to Developing Countries: The Policy Alternatives**
C. Fred Bergsten, William R. Cline, and John Williamson/*April 1985*
ISBN paper 0-88132-032-3 221 pp.

11 **Trading for Growth: The Next Round of Trade Negotiations**
Gary Clyde Hufbauer and Jeffrey J. Schott/*September 1985*
(out of print) ISBN paper 0-88132-033-1 109 pp.

12 **Financial Intermediation Beyond the Debt Crisis**
Donald R. Lessard and John Williamson/*September 1985*
(out of print) ISBN paper 0-88132-021-8 130 pp.

13 **The United States-Japan Economic Problem**
C. Fred Bergsten and William R. Cline/*October 1985, 2d ed. January 1987*
(out of print) ISBN paper 0-88132-060-9 180 pp.

14 Deficits and the Dollar: The World Economy at Risk
Stephen Marris/*December 1985, 2d ed. November 1987*
(out of print) ISBN paper 0-88132-067-6 415 pp.

15 Trade Policy for Troubled Industries
Gary Clyde Hufbauer and Howard F. Rosen/*March 1986*
ISBN paper 0-88132-020-X 111 pp.

16 The United States and Canada: The Quest for Free Trade
Paul Wonnacott, with an Appendix by John Williamson/*March 1987*
ISBN paper 0-88132-056-0 188 pp.

17 Adjusting to Success: Balance of Payments Policy in the East Asian NICs
Bela Balassa and John Williamson/*June 1987, rev. April 1990*
ISBN paper 0-88132-101-X 160 pp.

18 Mobilizing Bank Lending to Debtor Countries
William R. Cline/*June 1987*
ISBN paper 0-88132-062-5 100 pp.

19 Auction Quotas and United States Trade Policy
C. Fred Bergsten, Kimberly Ann Elliott, Jeffrey J. Schott, and Wendy E. Takacs/*September 1987*
ISBN paper 0-88132-050-1 254 pp.

20 Agriculture and the GATT: Rewriting the Rules
Dale E. Hathaway/*September 1987*
ISBN paper 0-88132-052-8 169 pp.

21 Anti-Protection: Changing Forces in United States Trade Politics
I. M. Destler and John S. Odell/*September 1987*
ISBN paper 0-88132-043-9 220 pp.

22 Targets and Indicators: A Blueprint for the International Coordination of Economic Policy
John Williamson and Marcus H. Miller/*September 1987*
ISBN paper 0-88132-051-X 118 pp.

23 Capital Flight: The Problem and Policy Responses
Donald R. Lessard and John Williamson/*December 1987*
(out of print) ISBN paper 0-88132-059-5 80 pp.

24 United States-Canada Free Trade: An Evaluation of the Agreement
Jeffrey J. Schott/*April 1988*
ISBN paper 0-88132-072-2 48 pp.

25 Voluntary Approaches to Debt Relief
John Williamson/*September 1988, rev. May 1989*
ISBN paper 0-88132-098-6 80 pp.

26 American Trade Adjustment: The Global Impact
William R. Cline/*March 1989*
ISBN paper 0-88132-095-1 98 pp.

27 More Free Trade Areas?
Jeffrey J. Schott/*May 1989*
ISBN paper 0-88132-085-4 88 pp.

28 The Progress of Policy Reform in Latin America
John Williamson/*January 1990*
ISBN paper 0-88132-100-1 106 pp.

29 **The Global Trade Negotiations: What Can Be Achieved?**
Jeffrey J. Schott/*September 1990*
ISBN paper 0-88132-137-0 72 pp.

30 **Economic Policy Coordination: Requiem or Prologue?**
Wendy Dobson/*April 1991*
ISBN paper 0-88132-102-8 162 pp.

31 **The Economic Opening of Eastern Europe**
John Williamson/*May 1991*
ISBN paper 0-88132-186-9 92 pp.

32 **Eastern Europe and the Soviet Union in the World Economy**
Susan M. Collins and Dani Rodrik/*May 1991*
ISBN paper 0-88132-157-5 152 pp.

33 **African Economic Reform: The External Dimension**
Carol Lancaster/*June 1991*
ISBN paper 0-88132-096-X 82 pp.

34 **Has the Adjustment Process Worked?**
Paul R. Krugman/*October 1991*
ISBN paper 0-88132-116-8 80 pp.

35 **From Soviet disUnion to Eastern Economic Community?**
Oleh Havrylyshyn and John Williamson/*October 1991*
ISBN paper 0-88132-192-3 84 pp.

36 **Global Warming: The Economic Stakes**
William R. Cline/*May 1992*
ISBN paper 0-88132-172-9 128 pp.

37 **Trade and Payments After Soviet Disintegration**
John Williamson/*June 1992*
ISBN paper 0-88132-173-7 96 pp.

38 **Trade and Migration: NAFTA and Agriculture**
Philip L. Martin/*October 1993*
ISBN paper 0-88132-201-6 160 pp.

39 **The Exchange Rate System and the IMF: A Modest Agenda**
Morris Goldstein/*June 1995*
ISBN paper 0-88132-219-9 104 pp.

40 **What Role for Currency Boards?**
John Williamson/*September 1995*
ISBN paper 0-88132-222-9 64 pp.

41 **Predicting External Imbalances for the United States and Japan**
William R. Cline/*September 1995*
ISBN paper 0-88132-220-2 104 pp.

BOOKS

IMF Conditionality
John Williamson, editor/*1983*
ISBN cloth 0-88132-006-4 695 pp.

Trade Policy in the 1980s
William R. Cline, editor/*1983*
(out of print) ISBN cloth 0-88132-008-1 810 pp.
ISBN paper 0-88132-031-5 810 pp.

Subsidies in International Trade
Gary Clyde Hufbauer and Joanna Shelton Erb/*1984*
ISBN cloth 0-88132-004-8 299 pp.

International Debt: Systemic Risk and Policy Response
William R. Cline/*1984*
ISBN cloth 0-88132-015-3 336 pp.

Trade Protection in the United States: 31 Case Studies
Gary Clyde Hufbauer, Diane E. Berliner, and Kimberly Ann Elliott/*1986*
(out of print) ISBN paper 0-88132-040-4 371 pp.

Toward Renewed Economic Growth in Latin America
Bela Balassa, Gerardo M. Bueno, Pedro-Pablo Kuczynski, and Mario Henrique Simonsen/*1986*
(out of stock) ISBN paper 0-88132-045-5 205 pp.

Capital Flight and Third World Debt
Donald R. Lessard and John Williamson, editors/*1987*
(out of print) ISBN paper 0-88132-053-6 270 pp.

The Canada-United States Free Trade Agreement: The Global Impact
Jeffrey J. Schott and Murray G. Smith, editors/*1988*
ISBN paper 0-88132-073-0 211 pp.

World Agricultural Trade: Building a Consensus
William M. Miner and Dale E. Hathaway, editors/*1988*
ISBN paper 0-88132-071-3 226 pp.

Japan in the World Economy
Bela Balassa and Marcus Noland/*1988*
ISBN paper 0-88132-041-2 306 pp.

America in the World Economy: A Strategy for the 1990s
C. Fred Bergsten/*1988*
ISBN cloth 0-88132-089-7 235 pp.
ISBN paper 0-88132-082-X 235 pp.

Managing the Dollar: From the Plaza to the Louvre
Yoichi Funabashi/*1988, 2d ed. 1989*
ISBN paper 0-88132-097-8 307 pp.

United States External Adjustment and the World Economy
William R. Cline/*May 1989*
ISBN paper 0-88132-048-X 392 pp.

Free Trade Areas and U.S. Trade Policy
Jeffrey J. Schott, editor/*May 1989*
ISBN paper 0-88132-094-3 400 pp.

Dollar Politics: Exchange Rate Policymaking in the United States
I. M. Destler and C. Randall Henning/*September 1989*
(out of print) ISBN paper 0-88132-079-X 192 pp.

Latin American Adjustment: How Much Has Happened?
John Williamson, editor/*April 1990*
ISBN paper 0-88132-125-7 480 pp.

The Future of World Trade in Textiles and Apparel
William R. Cline/*1987, 2d ed. June 1990*
ISBN paper 0-88132-110-9 344 pp.

Completing the Uruguay Round: A Results-Oriented Approach to the GATT Trade Negotiations
Jeffrey J. Schott, editor/*September 1990*
ISBN paper 0-88132-130-3 256 pp.

Economic Sanctions Reconsidered (in two volumes)

Economic Sanctions Reconsidered: Supplemental Case Histories
Gary Clyde Hufbauer, Jeffrey J. Schott, and Kimberly Ann Elliott/*1985, 2d ed. December 1990*

	ISBN cloth 0-88132-115-X	928 pp.
	ISBN paper 0-88132-105-2	928 pp.

Economic Sanctions Reconsidered: History and Current Policy
Gary Clyde Hufbauer, Jeffrey J. Schott, and Kimberly Ann Elliott/*December 1990*

	ISBN cloth 0-88132-136-2	288 pp.
	ISBN paper 0-88132-140-0	288 pp.

Pacific Basin Developing Countries: Prospects for the Future
Marcus Noland/*January 1991*

(out of print)	ISBN cloth 0-88132-141-9	250 pp.
	ISBN paper 0-88132-081-1	250 pp.

Currency Convertibility in Eastern Europe
John Williamson, editor/*October 1991*

	ISBN cloth 0-88132-144-3	396 pp.
	ISBN paper 0-88132-128-1	396 pp.

International Adjustment and Financing: The Lessons of 1985-1991
C. Fred Bergsten, editor/*January 1992*

	ISBN paper 0-88132-112-5	336 pp.

North American Free Trade: Issues and Recommendations
Gary Clyde Hufbauer and Jeffrey J. Schott/*April 1992*

	ISBN cloth 0-88132-145-1	392 pp.
	ISBN paper 0-88132-120-6	392 pp.

Narrowing the U.S. Current Account Deficit
Allen J. Lenz/*June 1992*

(out of print)	ISBN cloth 0-88132-148-6	640 pp.
	ISBN paper 0-88132-103-6	640 pp.

The Economics of Global Warming
William R. Cline/*June 1992*

	ISBN cloth 0-88132-150-8	416 pp.
	ISBN paper 0-88132-132-X	416 pp.

U.S. Taxation of International Income: Blueprint for Reform
Gary Clyde Hufbauer, assisted by Joanna M. van Rooij/*October 1992*

	ISBN cloth 0-88132-178-8	304 pp.
	ISBN paper 0-88132-134-6	304 pp.

Who's Bashing Whom? Trade Conflict in High-Technology Industries
Laura D'Andrea Tyson/*November 1992*

	ISBN cloth 0-88132-151-6	352 pp.
	ISBN paper 0-88132-106-0	352 pp.

Korea in the World Economy
Il SaKong/*January 1993*

	ISBN cloth 0-88132-184-2	328 pp.
	ISBN paper 0-88132-106-0	328 pp.

Pacific Dynamism and the International Economic System
C. Fred Bergsten and Marcus Noland, editors/*May 1993*

	ISBN paper 0-88132-196-6	424 pp.

Economic Consequences of Soviet Disintegration
John Williamson, editor/*May 1993*
ISBN paper 0-88132-190-7 664 pp.

Reconcilable Differences? United States-Japan Economic Conflict
C. Fred Bergsten and Marcus Noland/*June 1993*
ISBN paper 0-88132-129-X 296 pp.

Does Foreign Exchange Intervention Work?
Kathryn M. Dominguez and Jeffrey A. Frankel/*September 1993*
ISBN paper 0-88132-104-4 192 pp.

Sizing Up U.S. Export Disincentives
J. David Richardson/*September 1993*
ISBN paper 0-88132-107-9 192 pp.

NAFTA: An Assessment
Gary Clyde Hufbauer and Jeffrey J. Schott/*rev. ed. October 1993*
ISBN paper 0-88132-199-0 216 pp.

Adjusting to Volatile Energy Prices
Philip K. Verleger, Jr./*November 1993*
ISBN paper 0-88132-069-2 288 pp.

The Political Economy of Policy Reform
John Williamson, editor/*January 1994*
ISBN paper 0-88132-195-8 624 pp.

Measuring the Costs of Protection in the United States
Gary Clyde Hufbauer and Kimberly Ann Elliott/*January 1994*
ISBN paper 0-88132-108-7 144 pp.

The Dynamics of Korean Economic Development
Cho Soon/*March 1994*
ISBN paper 0-88132-162-1 272 pp.

Reviving the European Union
C. Randall Henning, Eduard Hochreiter and Gary Clyde Hufbauer, editors/*April 1994*
ISBN paper 0-88132-208-3 192 pp.

China in the World Economy
Nicholas R. Lardy/*April 1994*
ISBN paper 0-88132-200-8 176 pp.

Greening the GATT: Trade, Environment, and the Future
Daniel C. Esty/ *July 1994*
ISBN paper 0-88132-205-9 344 pp.

Western Hemisphere Economic Integration
Gary Clyde Hufbauer and Jeffrey J. Schott/*July 1994*
ISBN paper 0-88132-159-1 304 pp.

Currencies and Politics in the United States, Germany, and Japan
C. Randall Henning/*September 1994*
ISBN paper 0-88132-127-3 432 pp.

Estimating Equilibrium Exchange Rates
John Williamson, editor/*September 1994*
ISBN paper 0-88132-076-5 320 pp.

Managing the World Economy: Fifty Years After Bretton Woods
Peter B. Kenen, editor/*September 1994*
ISBN paper 0-88132-212-1 448 pp.

Reciprocity and Retaliation in U.S. Trade Policy
Thomas O. Bayard and Kimberly Ann Elliott/*September 1994*
ISBN paper 0-88132-084-6 528 pp.

The Uruguay Round: An Assessment
Jeffrey J. Schott, assisted by Johanna W. Buurman/*November 1994*
ISBN paper 0-88132-206-7 240 pp.

Measuring the Costs of Protection in Japan
Yoko Sazanami, Shujiro Urata, and Hiroki Kawai/*January 1995*
ISBN paper 0-88132-211-3 96 pp.

Foreign Direct Investment in the United States, Third Edition
Edward M. Graham and Paul R. Krugman/*January 1995*
ISBN paper 0-88132-204-0 232 pp.

The Political Economy of Korea-United States Cooperation
C. Fred Bergsten and Il SaKong, editors/*February 1995*
ISBN paper 0-88132-213-X 128 pp.

International Debt Reexamined
William R. Cline/*February 1995*
ISBN paper 0-88132-083-8 560 pp.

American Trade Politics, Third Edition
I. M. Destler/*April 1995*
ISBN paper 0-88132-215-6 360 pp.

Managing Official Export Credits: The Quest for a Global Regime
John E. Ray/*July 1995*
ISBN paper 0-88132-207-5 344 pp.

SPECIAL REPORTS

1 **Promoting World Recovery: A Statement on Global Economic Strategy by Twenty-six Economists from Fourteen Countries**/*December 1982*
(out of print) ISBN paper 0-88132-013-7 45 pp.

2 **Prospects for Adjustment in Argentina, Brazil, and Mexico: Responding to the Debt Crisis**
John Williamson, editor/*June 1983*
(out of print) ISBN paper 0-88132-016-1 71 pp.

3 **Inflation and Indexation: Argentina, Brazil, and Israel**
John Williamson, editor/*March 1985*
ISBN paper 0-88132-037-4 191 pp.

4 **Global Economic Imbalances**
C. Fred Bergsten, editor/*March 1986*
ISBN cloth 0-88132-038-2 126 pp.
ISBN paper 0-88132-042-0 126 pp.

5 **African Debt and Financing**
Carol Lancaster and John Williamson, editors/*May 1986*
(out of print) ISBN paper 0-88132-044-7 229 pp.

6 **Resolving the Global Economic Crisis: After Wall Street**
Thirty-three Economists from Thirteen Countries/*December 1987*
ISBN paper 0-88132-070-6 30 pp.

7 **World Economic Problems**
Kimberly Ann Elliott and John Williamson, editors/*April 1988*
ISBN paper 0-88132-055-2 298 pp.

Reforming World Agricultural Trade
Twenty-nine Professionals from Seventeen Countries/*1988*
ISBN paper 0-88132-088-9 42 pp.

8 **Economic Relations Between the United States and Korea: Conflict or Cooperation?**
Thomas O. Bayard and Soo-Gil Young, editors/*January 1989*
ISBN paper 0-88132-068-4 192 pp.

WORKS IN PROGRESS

The list below describes research in progress at the Institute. It is intended to inform our customers about our current research agenda. We do not accept back orders for books in this section because of the uncertainty about publication dates.

Global Firms and National Governments
Edward M. Graham

Mismanaging the World Economy: The Demise of the G7
C. Fred Bergsten and C. Randall Henning

Trade, Jobs, and Income Distribution
William R. Cline

Trade and Labor Standards
Kimberly Ann Elliott and Richard Freeman

Regionalism and Globalism in the World Economic System
Jeffrey A. Frankel

Asia-Pacific Fusion: Japan's Role in APEC
Yoichi Funabashi

Overseeing Global Capital Markets
Morris Goldstein and Peter Garber

Global Competition Policy
Edward M. Graham and J. David Richardson

Border Tax Adjustment
Gary Clyde Hufbauer

Toward an Asia Pacific Economic Community?
Gary Clyde Hufbauer and Jeffrey J. Schott

The Economics of Korean Unification
Marcus Noland

The Case for Trade: A Modern Reconsideration
J. David Richardson

The Future of the World Trading System
John Whalley, in collaboration with Colleen Hamilton

Standards and Conformity Assessment in APEC
John Wilson

For orders outside the US and Canada please contact:

Longman Group UK Ltd.
PO Box 88
Fourth Avenue
Harlow, Essex CM 19 5SR UK

Telephone Orders: 0279 623923
Fax: 0279 453450
Telex: 81259

Canadian customers can order from the Institute or from either:

RENOUF BOOKSTORE
1294 Algoma Road
Ottawa, Ontario K1B 3W8
Telephone: (613) 741-4333
Fax: (613) 741-5439

LA LIBERTÉ
3020 chemin Sainte-Foy
Quebec G1X 3V6
Telephone: (418) 658-3763
Fax: (800) 567-5449